GLOBETR

Travel

SEYCHELLES

Paul Tingay

Windsor and Maidenhead

Garfield House, 86 Edgware Road
London W2 2EA
United Kingdom

Wembley Square, First Floor, Solan Road
Gardens, Cape Town 8001
South Africa

Unit 1, 66 Gibbes Street,
Chatswood NSW 2067
Australia

218 Lake Road
Northcote, Auckland
New Zealand

Distributed in the USA by
The Globe Pequot Press, Connecticut

ISBN 978 1 78009 387 1

Keep us Current
Information in travel guides is apt to change, which is why
we regularly update our guides. We'd be grateful to receive
feedback if you've noticed something we should include in
our updates. If you have new information, please share it
with us by writing to the Publishing Manager, Globetrotter,
at the office nearest to you (addresses on this page). The
most significant contribution to each new edition will
receive a free copy of the updated guide.

...laar
...né Hart
...Bouwer, Mary Duncan,

..., Lyndall Hamilton
...cks, Reneé Spocter,

3983722

...Inga Nalbongo, Nicole Bannister

Picture Researcher: Shavonne Govender
Reproduction by Hirt & Carter (Cape) Cape Town
Printed and bound by Craft Print International Ltd, Singapore

Acknowledgements: The publishers and author would
like to thank Alan, Mickey and Kathy Mason, and Mifa
Monthy, all of Seychelles. Also, André Rassool, and
Georges and Margaret Norah.

Photographic credits:
Travel Pictures Ltd., cover; **Anthony Bannister**, page 81;
Anthony Bannister/IOA, page 15; **Camerapix**, pages 49,
67; **Martin Harvey**, pages 13, 99, 102, 111, 116, 118,
119, 120, 121; **Images of Africa (IOA)**, page 34;
Stefania Lamberti, pages 83, 112, 115; **Buddy Mays**,
pages 92, 114; **Fiona McIntosh/IOA**, pages 50, 72, 88;
Ian Michler, page 9; **Gilbert Pool** (courtesy Paul Tingay),
page 16; **Alain Proust**, page 32; **South African Library**,
page 22; **Paul Tingay**, title page; pages 4, 6, 8, 10, 11,
12, 14, 17, 18, 19, 20, 21, 23, 25, 26, 27, 28, 29, 30,
31, 33, 35, 36, 38, 39, 41, 42, 43, 45, 47, 48, 51, 52,
53, 56, 59, 60, 61, 62, 63, 64, 65, 66, 68, 69, 75, 76,
77, 78, 79, 82, 84, 85, 91, 93, 94, 95, 96, 98, 105, 106,
107, 109, 110, 113, 122.

Front cover: Anse Source d'Argent, La Digue Island.
Title page: Baie Chevalier and Anse Lazio beach, Praslin.

CONTENTS

1
Introducing Seychelles

The soaring mountains of Seychelles, covered with lush jungle, emerge from deep blue seas and a hundred glistening reefs. These Indian Ocean islands, numbering 115 in all, stretch in a jewelled crescent from the equator to the tip of Madagascar. With a population of just over 90,000 Kreol-speaking inhabitants, whose ancestors came from Africa, Arabia, India, Europe, Persia and even China, Seychelles was unknown until the airport sprung the Aladdin's Cave of tourism.

Many of the islands are tiny palm-tufted coral specks where yours may be the only yacht to weigh anchor in a year. **Aldabra**, the world's largest atoll and a World Heritage Site, is home to 150,000 giant tortoises. In the high mist forests of **Mahé** and **Silhouette** there are bats that eat mangoes, pitcher plants that gobble insects, and pygmy piping frogs the size of an emerald. The extraordinary beauty of the islands is such that nearly half of Seychelles' landmass has been set aside as national park.

Mahé, the main island, is a Bali Hai of sweeping beaches, jungle mountains and secluded coves. Tales of buried pirate treasure abound and elderly plantation houses decay away under breadfruit trees. On neighbouring **Praslin**, the presence of giant male and female coco de mer palms has given Seychelles its exotic reputation as the islands of love. Catamaran fastboats call at **La Digue**, where oxcarts trundle along the roads. Some islands are strictly for the birds, others have a solitary, luxury lodge, while many seem to be no more than a mirage across the wide ocean.

INNER ISLANDS — Aride, Curieuse, Cousin, North Island, Praslin, Félicité, La Digue, Silhouette, Victoria, Mahé, Frégate

TOP ATTRACTIONS

★★★ **Beau Vallon Beach, Mahé:** a classic sweep of sand, waves, and chunky takamaka trees.
★★★ **Morne Seychellois National Park:** a mountainous living museum of exotic birds and plants.
★★ **Vallée de Mai, Praslin:** the home of the unique coco de mer forest.
★★ **Ste Anne Marine National Park:** exquisite fish and corals close to Mahé.
★★ **Denis and Bird Islands:** sea birds, lush forest, emerald seas.
★ **La Digue:** take the catamaran or schooner ferry service from Praslin to the most traditional of the main islands.

◀ *Opposite: Palms, surf and hidden coves.*

5

- **World's largest tortoise**: there are 150,000 giant land tortoises on Aldabra. They weigh up to 150kg (330lb) and stand half a metre high.
- **Heaviest fruit**: the double nut of the coco de mer palm weighs 18kg (40lb), making it the heaviest fruit in the plant kingdom.
- **Rarest tree**: the jellyfish tree. Once thought to be extinct, there are no more than 50 in the world, all in Mahé's mountains.
- **Largest fish**: the world's largest and harmless fish is the whale shark, a frequent visitor to the islands' coral reefs.
- **Wide-eyed bat**: the Seychelles fruit bat not only eats fruit, but it can see well.
- **Granite isles**: most mid-oceanic islands in the world are formed by coral. The Inner Islands of Seychelles are the tips of continental granite mountains.

THE LAND

Millions of years ago as fires burned and melted in the bowels of the earth, the supercontinent of Gondwana, which included much of the southern hemisphere, tore itself apart. India separated from Africa, the sea rushed in to fill gaping canyons, and deserts and plains were covered by fathomless ocean. It was a process that spanned aeons and embraced the genesis of countless new species of life on earth. Gradually the seasons settled to a gentler rhythm, and the continents assumed their familiar shapes. Left in the middle of the Indian Ocean after this awesome cataclysm were the tips of some of the highest mountains and a hundred isolated coral atolls, a necklace of pearls in a forgotten sea, islands that we now know as Seychelles.

The Granitic Islands

Scattered across some 400,000km² (154,000 sq miles) of sea in the western Indian Ocean, the islands of Seychelles are made up of two distinct geological types: coralline and granitic. Most mid-oceanic islands in the world are formed from coral and volcanic action; the exceptions are the Inner Islands of the Seychelles, which are the remnants of continental Gondwanaland.

Mahé, the largest island, together with **Praslin**, **La Digue**, **Silhouette** and the other granitic islands closest to them, account for nearly 50% of the Seychelles' land-

mass. These are the islands where most Seychellois live, and where the majority of visitor facilities are located. They are all situated in a tight group in the northeastern part of the archipelago, 1600km (1000 miles) from Africa. Apart from towering black granite cliffs high in the mountains and the sensuous, sculptured boulders

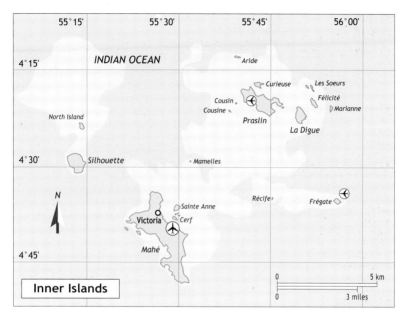

Inner Islands

that frame many deserted beaches, the granitic islands give the impression of being covered in impenetrable jungle. Mahé's mountainous Morne Seychellois National Park is a wilderness of tangled tropical splendour, but much of the greenery also comes from the profusion of coconut palms, wild cinnamon, and graceful *albizia* trees.

Mahé's beaches and coves are a continuous delight. They all have palms and gnarled *takamaka* trees shading them, the water is crystal clear and the swimming safe. A few hundred metres in front of most beaches are long lines of rumbling white water at the edge of the reef. The coastline is dotted with airy bungalows, each village with its own church bell tower, crowded general store and small guesthouses.

Some 40km (25 miles) east of Mahé and constantly visible as a blue ridge on the horizon, the second-largest island, Praslin, hides the fabled coco de mer palm in its forested hills. La Digue, near Praslin, has one village,

◄ *Opposite: A cascade of granite 500 million years old.*

NATIONAL SYMBOLS

- The Seychelles coat of arms displays two sailfish and a tropicbird around a crest which includes a tortoise, a coco de mer, a schooner, and a green island.
- The national flower is the tropicbird orchid.
- The national bird is the Seychelles black parrot (it's actually brown), the only parrot on the islands.
- Air Seychelles' logo displays twin snowy white fairy terns in flight.

▲ *Above: An aerial view of Bird Island.*

Gregoire's supermarket, and unique pink-tinged granite boulders among an abundance of palms and delightful little coves. Silhouette, the third-largest island, is to most people a mist-shrouded peak visible from Mahé's Beau Vallon Beach. Other smaller granitic islands (some are resorts) are dispersed around the larger ones, a number of them bird and nature sanctuaries.

The Coralline Islands

The 74 coral islands and atolls of Seychelles are the far-flung outposts of the group. They make up 47% of the land area of the Seychelles, yet only a thousand of the islands' population of 90,000 live on them. During the last Ice Age the level of the Indian Ocean was much lower and there were thousands more, including now-submerged fishing banks.

Denis Island and **Bird Island**, both coral islands, are normally grouped with the Inner Islands. The rest – tiny, horizon-floating islands tufted with palms – are collectively called the Outer Islands, or *zil elwayen* in Kreol, and are spread out like diamond dust across a vast expanse of ocean.

Many of them are only 3m (10ft) above sea level. Some islands have remote lagoons; all have windswept palms, talcum beaches and magical underwater gardens. **Aldabra** and **Farquhar**, the furthest from Mahé, each have a dozen islands, and the **Amirantes** group, named after the Portuguese explorer Admiral Vasco da Gama, twice that. Aldabra atoll, a ring of ferociously pitted limestone coral enclosing a lagoon 34km (21 miles) across, is a World Heritage Site and home to 150,000 giant tortoises, 2000 breeding turtles, and huge, tree-climbing crabs.

Ocean and Reef

The Indian Ocean dominates the Seychelles, whether by the immense depth of water just beyond the reefs, the influence of the oceanic weather patterns, or simply in the vast distances between the little specks of islands. Most visitors will come into contact with the ocean in some form or another: swimming in the warm, protected waters, or sailing on a schooner between the islands. Where meeting the ocean really becomes special, however, is underwater, diving and snorkelling on the edges of a vast new world of coral, waving polyps, fish, and overwhelming silence.

▲ *Above: Snorkelling is a popular pastime in the crystal coral waters of the Seychelles.*

After millions of years sitting in the ocean, even the granite islands have attracted a ring of coral around their shores. Coral atolls and islands are normally the result of coral growing around a geological formation, such as a volcano, which has sunk into the sea, leaving the crust of coral in place. Coral is a living force, always growing, changing, and offering life to a vast chain of sea creatures, from minute plankton to a myriad flashing fish, porpoises and whales that find the waters of Seychelles so attractive.

Off some shores in the islands the reef is close to the shore and exposed at low tide, which makes for fascinating exploration, while along the beaches themselves you will always be able to find the scattered, delicate artistry of shells and dead coral.

SEYCHELLES	J	F	M	A	M	J	J	A	S	O	N	D
MAX TEMP. °C	30	30	31	32	31	28	29	29	29	30	30	30
MIN TEMP. °C	25	25	26	26	26	25	24	25	25	25	25	25
MAX TEMP. °F	86	86	88	90	88	82	84	84	84	86	86	86
MIN TEMP. °F	77	77	79	79	79	77	75	77	77	77	77	77
RAINFALL mm	541	177	249	168	81	158	52	93	300	246	217	335
RAINFALL in	21	7	10	7	3	6	2	4	12	10	9	13
DAYS OF RAINFALL	12	15	15	14	14	12	12	11	12	13	17	19

▲ *Above: A young female coco de mer tree.*

Climate

Seychelles lies in the tropics between 4° and 10°S of the equator. The average daily **temperature** is 29°C (84°F), the average **humidity** a steamy 80% and there are about seven hours of **sunshine** daily. The refreshing southeast **trade winds** blow from April to October, when the weather tends to be cooler and drier, while the lighter northwest monsoon winds arrive during the Christmas period. At this time the **rain** can fall in torrential downpours, but there are short, showery spells any time of year. The force of the tropical showers means that the annual rainfall is around 2500mm (99in), which is nearly four times that of London. However, being small islands in a wide ocean, Seychelles' many microclimates ensure conditions are very localized – it can be raining on one beach, sunny on the next and misty up in the mountains.

The islands are at their windiest from April to September, which are the best sailing months. The coral islands are drier, warmer and, being at sea level, usually catch refreshing sea breezes. Only Farquhar atoll is within the storm winds cyclone belt.

Plant Life

The shoreline of the main granitic islands was once a jungle of almost impenetrable 30m (100ft) tall hardwood trees, but settlement, naval rivalry during the Napoleonic wars and plantations soon devastated those. Even today, however, the impression is still of a botanic riot of dense breadfruit trees, flame trees,

LULU THE GHOST CRAB

Trouloulou, in Kreol, the ghost crab, is the mischievous thief of the sands. It preys on hatchling turtles and is in turn preyed upon by fishermen who use these delicate sand dancers as bait. Lulu is hilarious to watch, particularly at night, peak revelry time, as she skitters in jerkstart six-by-six sprints across a pristine moonlit beach. Frightened, she will hunker down pretending to be invisible, then rush on tiny tiptoes for burrow or surf.

banyans and bananas, and everywhere an unwelcome creeper called Lalayann d'Argent or elephant climber. Old coconut and cinnamon plantations are everywhere, and wild fruits grow in every back yard: mangoes, bananas, tamarinds, star-shaped *karambol*, fluffy fruited *prunes de France*, and prickly *frisiter*. Alongside the requisite palms on every beach there are shading *takamaka* and casuarina trees, whose tiny cones create a minefield for barefoot bathers. Among the 103 tree and plant species unique to Seychelles are the wild *bilenbi*, whose tart fruit actually grows on the trunk of the tree, and possibly the rarest tree on earth, the *bwa mediz* or jellyfish tree. Lost to botanists since 1908, its rediscovery 60 years later caused quite a stir at Kew Gardens in London. There are only about 50 in the world, all in the high mountains of Mahé. It is a bushy, rather unspectacular tree, which takes its name, jellyfish, from its umbrella-shaped fruit. A total of 1108 species of plants grow in Seychelles of which 257 flourish mainly in the coralline islands and 85 are ferns. Shore plants include shiny green *veloutier*, casuarinas, coconuts and hardy mangroves.

Lording over the botanical castle, however, is the giant **coco de mer** coconut palm, whose male catkins and double female nuts bear a striking resemblance to the respective human reproductive organs. The Vallée de Mai nature reserve on Praslin Island is the largest natural preserve of these monster palms which are endemic to (i.e. they originate uniquely from) Seychelles.

Creatures of Land, Sea and Air

Seychelles may once have been linked to Africa and India but it has no big game. The only endemic mammals in residence are the 1m wingspan fruit bats, among them the giant fruit bat which, unlike other bats, can see.

Giant land tortoises are only found in two places in the world: the Galapagos islands off South America, and Seychelles. They grow up to half a metre (1.6ft) high, weigh 150kg (330lb)

COCO DE MER

In Seychelles much ado is made about this huge double-nutted coconut that legend suggests might have been the Tree of Knowledge in the Garden of Eden.
● World's largest nut. Up to 20kg (44lb).
● World's largest leaves. Up to 6m (20ft) span.
● The trees stand a towering 30m (100ft) tall.
● Maximum age 220 years. Some say 1000 years. Today's trees were young shoots when the first French settlers arrived in 1770.
● Some 3000 numbered souvenir nuts are sold annually.
● Eve would have found it difficult to bite through the husk of the coco de mer. It is 10cm (4in) thick. The opaque jelly-like fruit of this unique tree, possibly pollinated by lizards, is used in Chinese cuisine, but raw it tastes like Armageddon.

▼ *Below: Blue-black beak and mischievous eyes characterize the Seychelles fairy tern.*

Seychelles has set aside nearly half its land area, or 208km² (80 sq miles) as national park and protected reserve. And, appropriately for a nation of islands, almost the same area has been designated for marine parks. The principal areas are:

• **Morne Seychellois National Park**, on Mahé. Walking trails up through the unique forest to mountain viewpoints.

• **Praslin National Park**. All six endemic palms (including the coco de mer in the Vallée de Mai).

• **Aride Island**. A Special Reserve to the north of Praslin. Birds everywhere and the highest density of reptiles in the world.

• **Cousin Island**. Another Special Reserve. Sea birds galore and the largest breeding population of hawksbill turtles in Seychelles.

• **Ste Anne Marine National Park**. This lovely park opposite Mahé is under threat from reclaimed land developers, as is Félicité Island.

• **Curieuse Island Marine Park**. A park of land and sea off the north coast of Praslin.

and at least some are believed to be 200 years old. The ancient Greeks thought tortoises, *tartaroukhos*, came from the underworld; hence their name. There are five types of frogs in the islands, croaking in competitive concert in the mountains. The female tree frog grows up to 20cm (8in), somewhat overshadowing her spouse, who measures a mere 5cm (2in). After the early extermination of the Nile crocodiles, the only other land reptiles are geckos, skinks and a large endemic chameleon. The bright emerald green gecko will shed its wriggling tail as a ruse to distract an advancing predator.

There are 3500 insect species in Seychelles, most unique to the islands, including Frégate Island's giant tenebrionid beetle, and the Seychelles leaf insect, whose camouflage drag far outclasses the African variety. There are surprisingly few butterflies in Seychelles other than on the islands of the Aldabra group.

Millions of birds migrate from as far as the Arctic Circle to the coral islands of Seychelles to breed. Some of the islands, such as Aride and Cousine, host some spectacular and noisy colonies of sea birds, including noddies, terns and frigate birds. A number of land varieties are unique to Seychelles, and are constantly under threat of extinction. Amongst these are the Magpie Robin, Seychelles kestrel, blue pigeon, bulbul, the beautiful black paradise flycatcher, and the whistling black parrot of the coco de mer palms on Praslin.

▶ *Right: A giant tortoise, often confused with and closely related to the turtle,* ▶▶ *Opposite. Both animals are found in Seychelles. The turtle has a flatter shell, and its legs have developed into paddle-like flippers.*

Sea Life

Dolphins, whales and manta rays are all common in Seychelles waters. The dugong or sea cow was once here too and is remembered in the original name for Bird Island, Île aux Vaches (Isle of Cows). The larger sharks usually stay in deep waters, although the plankton-feeding whale shark, the largest fish in the world, is sometimes encountered by divers. The marine turtle nests

on a number of the islands, though nowadays all four species in Seychelles – green, hawksbill, loggerhead, and the giant leatherback – are continuously hunted by that relentless predator, man, and are carefully monitored and protected. Fighting fish such as marlin and under-threat tuna are caught in the waters around the islands. The most beautiful is the sailfish, which will leap out of the water shivering its silvery blue body in the sun.

Along the coral reefs there are a thousand flashing, darting and amazingly colourful reef fish. In the underwater forest you will see angelfish, parrotfish, cave-defending moray eels, hovering trumpetfish and the occasional turtle winging away in fright. There are black spiky urchins, tiger cowries, half-metre long crayfish and, occasionally, the protected *triton* conch shell blown by fishermen in early days to announce fish for sale.

Conserve with Care

Although 46% of Seychelles land area is protected in one form or another, it often seems as if the whole of Seychelles is one large and extraordinarily beautiful park: island and beach, mountain and forest, reef and ocean.

The 18ha (45-acre) **Vallée de Mai** on Praslin, the home of the coco de mer palms, is one of Seychelles' two World Heritage Sites. The other is the 34km (21-mile) long **Aldabra** atoll, with its giant tortoises, rare birds and green

DEVIL OF THE DEEP

The plankton-eating manta ray, or *diable de mer*, does not deserve its demonic name, for you cannot find a more graceful and harmless creature in the warm tropical waters. They look like stealth bombers, their pectoral wings spanning up to 7m (23ft), often in flights of six or more. They can weigh as much as 1300kg (2900lb). Seychelles fishermen used to harpoon them from small craft, but the manta is powerful and will easily drag a boat. The devil-fish tag comes from the hornlike fins on either side of its head. In the days of slavery, plantation owners were fond of whips made from manta tail.

INTRODUCING SEYCHELLES

DOOMED TURTLES

Not long ago turtles from the outer islands would be stacked like boxes on the decks of ships, and, crying and sighing all the while, transported to the Long Pier pool on Mahé to be slaughtered for steaks, salted *kitouz*, and the calipee (fat) used in Europe to make turtle soup. Their yellow ping-pong-ball eggs were also stolen to make cakes. They have survived for over 100 million years yet now are threatened with extinction. In times past 6000 green turtles were caught annually in Cosmoledo. Today in neighbouring Aldabra there are only 2000 breeding females left. Fortunately they are slowly increasing in numbers, but turtles are still hunted in Seychelles, proof that more needs to be done by a caring government, if time is not to turn turtle on these gentle creatures.

▼ *Below: A pirogue fisherman where nowadays jets come in to land.*

turtle breeding grounds. Tiny **Cousin Island** is administered by Nature Seychelles, while its sibling **Cousine** is a privately funded nature conservancy. Not too far away on La Digue Island the small **La Veuve Reserve** is trying with some success to conserve and nurture 100 of the last 250 individuals of long-tailed Seychelles black paradise flycatchers, one of the most threatened birds in the world.

Sea birds may not be disturbed on nine designated islands and spear fishing is prohibited everywhere. The collecting of live shells and corals is taboo and they may not be exported. Tragically both – from Southeast Asia – sell openly in Mahé. On some of the islands where the tree populations were devastated by plantations, reforestation schemes have been introduced. A number of transplantation schemes are being attempted for trees, birds, and even tortoises. The ceiling placed on the number of hotel beds by government some time ago is today subject to continuous pressure from foreign investors and government's perceived need to generate forex. This could gradually gnaw at the island's unique and fragile ecosystem.

HISTORY IN BRIEF

The Indian Ocean is the birthplace of long-distance sailing. Ancient Indian, Egyptian and Chinese texts, even DNA, indicate that there was sea-borne trade between India, China and Africa as long ago as 2000BCE. Polynesians setting out from the Bay of Bengal on their great canoes sailed east into the Pacific, and Indonesians west to the Maldives and Madagascar. The Phoenicians are

known to have rounded the southern tip of Africa and Indian sailors commissioned by the kings of Gujerat in the 6th century were colonizing Java, Bali and Madagascar. It is more than likely that some of these intrepid sailors stumbled upon the tiny mid-oceanic islands of the Seychelles on their voyages, possibly taking a little time to explore them, catch a turtle that offered some longed-for fresh meat, and perhaps plant a few crops to sustain them, before disappearing on their way again over the blue horizon.

Dhows in the Sea of Zanj

The first written record of the Seychelles (there may be Chinese texts still unearthed) dates from CE851, a time when Arab merchant seamen from the Persian Gulf in their lateen-rigged dhows made good use of the January winds blowing from India towards Africa, and then the opposite southeast monsoon a few months later, to navigate the ocean they called the Sea of Zanj, or Sea of Blacks.

In CE916, the geographer Abu Zaid al Hassan referred to the 'high islands beyond the Maldives', which is generally considered to be a reference to the uniquely mountainous Seychelles. The Arabs called the granitic Inner Islands of the Seychelles 'Zarin', or Sisters – a possible reference to the seven sisters of the Pleiades constellation – and as they are known to have brought the first coconut palm from India to the East African coast they may well have introduced it to Seychelles too. It is also clear that the coco de mer (which is endemic to Seychelles) was valued by Indian and Maldivan princes. At Anse Lascars on Silhouette and on Frégate Island there are Arab graves and ruins of coral brick buildings.

Chinese and Portuguese Pioneers

Five hundred years ago, soon after a huge Chinese fleet had abandoned the Indian Ocean for good, tiny Portuguese caravels under the command of **Vasco da Gama** braved storms and scurvy to journey around the Cape of Good Hope towards India and Japan. The

THE ROC

Arab sailors believed the Seychelles to be the islands of the mythological *rukh*, or giant roc bird. The legends said that the coco de mer tree grew up from beneath the ocean (hence its name – coco de mer, or coconut of the sea), and its branches provided a roosting place for the mighty bird with its 45m (150ft) wingspan which could carry off elephants, and would surely do the same to any sailor who came too close. Marco Polo recounted this tale to Kublai Khan in China 700 years ago, who immediately dispatched an envoy with instructions to return with a quill from the fabulous bird.

Amirantes Islands of the Seychelles, or the 'Isles of the Admiral', were named in 1502 in honour of Da Gama's promotion to the rank, but these first Europeans were not destined to settle on any of the islands they encountered. Within a few years the Portuguese had destroyed the Arab trade stranglehold on the Indian Ocean, and Portuguese names now dot the ocean map: Chagos, Comoros, Rodrigues, Agalega, Diego Garcia and Cosmoledo, the latter atoll a part of Seychelles.

Surveys, Spices, and Settlements

The first Englishmen to visit the islands that were to become their colony did so in 1609, with diarist **John Jourdain** giving us the first detailed picture of Seychelles. A hundred years later English and American pirates, harried out of the Caribbean, turned their swashbuckling attentions from the Spanish Main to the trade of spices, silks, tea and timber that was crisscrossing the Indian Ocean. Famous buccaneers such as **Captain Kidd, 'Long John' Avery**, **George Taylor**, and hook-nosed **Olivier le Vasseur** (known as *La Buze*, the Buzzard) roamed the lucrative seas, and found the deserted coves of Seychelles ideal places to hide, careen ships and bury plunder.

A rusty old anchor at Anse Boileau beach on Mahé marks the spot where French Captain **Lazare Picault** landed in 1742 to survey the Seychelles for Governor Mahé de Labourdonnais of Mauritius. He gave the island the name Île d'Abondance, and only later Mahé, in honour of his superior. Fourteen years were to pass before Commander **Corneille Nicholas Morphey** (of Irish-French descent) laid the official Stone of Possession

on the shore of Victoria harbour, and – astutely for an aspiring naval officer – renamed the group of islands Séchelles after the French finance minister.

The French authorities in Île de France (Mauritius), nervous of British colonial ambitions, were keen to back up their claim with actual occupancy, and so in 1770, encouraged by **Pierre Poivre**, an administrator of Île de France who thought Seychelles could rival the Dutch East Indies in the cultivation of spices, the first tiny party of settlers landed on Ste Anne's Island.

A small 'Etablissement du Roi', today's capital, Victoria, was built on Mahé, but the settlers grew few spices, and the colony survived rather than prospered.

Cannonballs and Capitulations

The French Revolution in 1789 set off a series of reactions around Europe that led to 20 years of war and the rise and fall of Napoleon. By 1794, when a new Commandant **Chevalier Jean-Baptiste Queau de Quinssy** arrived in the islands, Britain and France were at war, and the Indian Ocean was of growing strategic importance. The Seychelles were still in theory ruled from Mauritius, but they were remote and vulnerable.

On 16 May 1794, a squally day, when the island had been awake for a mere two hours, Commodore

---

THE BUZZARD'S BOOTY

The treasure of buccaneer Olivier le Vasseur is the most famous of the riches supposedly buried around the islands. The search has concentrated around Bel Ombre beach on Mahé, yet neither there, nor on any of the other islands around Seychelles where tantalizing tales of treasure abound, has anything beyond a few silver coins and a pistol or two ever been found. Or if there has, no-one is telling. Still, there is a Pirates Bay, a 'corsair' restaurant, a murdered buccaneer's tombstone in the National Museum, and a Pirates Arms hotel. Roman Polanski filmed *Il Pirato* in Seychelles. And what with a little yo ho ho and a bottle of local Takamaka Bay rum, it all makes sound tourism sense.

◄◄ *Opposite: An old French cannon harkens nostalgically for Napoleonic Empire days.*
◄ *Left: The lure of Seychelles from the time of the first settlers: coconuts, spices, and a marquetry box made from valuable local hardwoods.*

Henry Newcome of the British Royal Navy entered Victoria harbour, rather unsportingly flying a French flag. Faced by a combined British squadron firepower of 166 cannon and 12,500 trained men, De Quinssy remonstrated for honour's sake and then surrendered.

Down came the tricolor, up went the Union Jack, to a gentlemanly roll of drums and presentation of arms. Two weeks later the British sailed off, and the tricolor was back at the top of the flagpole with the *au revoirs* still ringing in the air. With alternate visits from French and British men o' war, De Quinssy became rather adept at welcoming first one side, then the other, supplying both with food, water, and a berth for repairs, while all the time acting as a refuge for French corsairs such as the notorious and dashing **Jean François Hodoul**.

Britain captured Mauritus (which still theoretically included the Seychelles) in 1810, but their only concern for the islands was that the enemy did not use them. The mercurial De Quinssy, showing typical political astuteness, anglicized his name to suit his new rulers, became De Quincy, and carried on as Chief Justice on Mahé until his death in 1827.

The Colonial Backwater

At this stage cotton, manioc and a dozen different spices were being grown by a population of 1800, of whom all but 300 were slaves. In 1835 slavery was abolished and

Seychelles was obliged to change from field husbandry to a total plantation economy (with crops such as coconuts, cinnamon, vanilla and patchouli) which did not require a large labour force. Former slaves were not interested in working on the plantations where, as they put it, 'the money is good, but too expensive'. The British

▶▶ *Opposite: A small farm at Anse Marie-Louise, Praslin, an area rich in coco de mer palms.*
▶ *Right: Jean François Hodoul, renowned gentleman corsair.*

adopted a policy of landing freed slaves on Seychelles (a total of 2500 over the years) where they were soon hired as labourers under 'apprenticeships', though with stinted rations, inadequate wages and rough treatment, their lives were hardly improved.

Saddled with a poor colony she did not want, Britain allowed Seychelles, for the rest of the 19th century and a good part of the next, to remain a peaceful, rather old-fashioned backwater visited by the occasional steamer and eccentric Victorian traveller. Among these were Marianne North, a botanist painter, and General 'Chinese' Gordon, who developed his quixotic theory of the biblical Genesis among the mysterious coco de mer palms of Praslin Island.

It was during the 19th century of splendid isolation and benign British laissez faire that the culture of Seychelles was formed – a mix of master and slave, planter and fisherman, France and Africa. Various crops and industries came and went over the years, including vanilla, copra, cinnamon, guano, and even whaling, but none seemed to last for long. The French farmers disliked their British rulers and in turn the British were disdainful. With the arrival in 1850 of the first Indian merchants and in 1895 a few Chinese, the Kreol kaleidoscope of the islands was complete.

The 20th Century

Seychelles eased gradually into the 20th century. In 1903 she emerged from under the skirts of Mauritius to take up status as a fully fledged colony. To mark this momentous development a Clock Tower was erected in the middle of Victoria, and for over 100 years it has been the centre of town and focus of traffic, business

SLAVERY

The first 21 settlers in 1770 on Ste Anne's Island included six slaves, and the economy of the islands was to depend on this cheap labour for the next 70 years. Slavery in the Seychelles was reasonably benevolent and not perhaps as harsh as in other parts of the world, but a person enslaved in the islands still suffered the threat of iron halter, chain and manta ray whip, along with appalling restrictions on movement, possessions, housing, marriage and the right to their children. Worst of all, perhaps, was the memory of abduction and the obliteration of cultural roots. To this day in Seychelles many appear reluctant to marry and the music of the islands, *moutya*, seems at times to reflect an indefinable loss and need for relationship and certainty.

In 1805 one Pierre Louis Poiret arrived in Seychelles. He always maintained (as did 40 others) that he was the legitimate heir to the French throne, son of Marie Antoinette and Louis XVI, and that he had been smuggled out of the Temple Prison in Paris and given as a child to a cobbler, whose name, Poiret, he took. Always deferred to with royal respect, he farmed on both Poivre and Mahé Islands and died at the age of 70 in 1856. Although never formally married, he left seven children, all of whom were named, in royal fashion, Louis or Louise.

and sophistication. In the islands, if you had not seen the *horloge* you were considered a country hick.

During these years, Indian indentured labourers built a road over the mountains to every visitor's favourite beach, Beau Vallon; Catholic churches and two secondary schools were established, and the British administration strived mightily and unsuccessfully to anglicize language and culture. The lovely iron-filigreed hospital near the Botanical Gardens was built: with elephantiasis, amoebic dysentery and leprosy it was much needed. The first car arrived, and in 1926 electricity hesitantly arrived to light the centre of town.

During World War II several contingents of Seychelles soldiers fought in the desert campaign. For many Seychellois it was the first taste of equality and freedom. Some stayed on in the British army, providing Rs650,000 in wages annually to 3000 poorer families. Their return in the early 1950s was a financial setback, but it was also the source of much excitement. 'Maman, the Tobruks have come back', the folk song went, 'what an occasion, Maman, I'll die or go mad if I don't find a husband.'

Immediately after the war **Dr (Sir) Percy Selwyn-Clarke**, medical officer in the notorious Japanese POW camp at Stanley in Hong Kong, became the first Governor appointed by a socialist government in London. 'I will have no colour bar in this colony', he declared, thus disenfranchising himself immediately in the esteem of the chattering classes down at **The Club**. Victoria's colourful fish and vegetable market is named after him.

A Tale of Two Lawyers

And it was time for politics. A taxpayers' association was formed and in 1940 the colonial legislative council permitted four elected

▼ Below: The Victoria Clock Tower, not long after it was erected to commemorate the granting of full colonial status to Seychelles in 1903.

◀ *Left: Multicoloured multi-styled buildings match the exotic mix of people and purchases in Market Street Mall, Victoria.*

members. In 1964, two political parties were formed: the Democratic Party, led by ebullient lawyer **James Mancham** (whose family ran a popular supermarket, Richards', in Victoria), and the broader based Seychelles People's United Party, also led by a lawyer, **Albert René**. For 40 turbulent years these two men remained at the centre of the country's political stage.

Universal adult suffrage arrived in 1967, but the great leap forward for Seychelles was to opt for tourism as the mainstay of the islands' economy. When the airport was constructed in 1971, the landing of the first VC10 was watched by practically the whole island.

Five years later, on 29 June 1976, Seychelles became independent from Britain and the bearded and Saville Row-besuited Mancham took over from the cockaded governor. Henceforth, two portraits adorned public buildings in Seychelles: one of the incumbent, President Mancham, and the other, with a leaner, somewhat hungrier look, of Prime Minister René.

The following year, while James Mancham was at a Commonwealth Conference in London, René pounced with a coup d'état. With Tanzanian troops standing by in Dar es Salaam as a backup, his men took the broadcasting centre, the police station and power. Three men were

EXILES IN EDEN

After an assassination attempt, Napoleon decided to banish 76 Jacobin 'terrorists' to Seychelles. The practice was to become quite established.

- 1877 **Sultan Abdullah of Perak**, whose successor spent his boyhood on Mahé and composed a song which for a while became the islands' national anthem.
- 1900 **King Prempeh II of Ashanti West Africa**, who arrived dressed in leopard skins, accompanied by his favourite executioner.
- 1916 **Seyyid Khalid bin Barghash of Zanzibar**, sent to Seychelles for being friendly to the Kaiser.
- In 1922 Winston Churchill considered sending 500 **Irish political prisoners** to Praslin.
- 1956 **Archbishop Makarios of Cyprus**; he stayed a year, was reputed to sing well, and enjoyed his Cypriot wine.
- 1981 **Failed coup d'etat** by mercenaries disguised as South African rugby players, 'Ye Ancient Order of Froth-Blowers'. Those caught were later forgiven.

▲ Above: James Mancham (right), the country's first president, and Albert René (left), then prime minister, seal an independence deal with Britain in 1976. Both ex-presidents live in Seychelles.

killed, one – an insurgent – became a hero while the other – a policeman – did not. Guns appeared in the streets, a curfew was announced, arrests were made and a people's militia formed. The revolution for *liberté, égalité, fraternité* had taken place, but as René was the people's choice anyway, history may well decide that it was unnecessary.

The Modern Era

Changes came quickly in the next two decades. It was, for the Seychellois, the best of times, the worst of times. Tourism soared, the economy boomed, construction flourished. New schools, old-age homes and health facilities all arrived. A confident spirit of nationhood fired *le peuple*, who soon became well nourished, well clothed, educated and employed. But it was also a time of counter-coups, plots and fear. In 1981 a planeload of South African mercenaries, led by 'Mad' Mike Hoare and joined by out-of-work Rhodesian Selous Scouts, launched an abortive invasion masquerading as a

HISTORICAL CALENDAR

250 million years ago The supercontinent of Gondwana splits up, leaving a few islands in the Indian Ocean. Among them, Seychelles.
2000BCE – CE500 Chinese, Egyptian, Indian, Greek, Roman and Phoenician explorations of the Indian Ocean. Some probably visit Seychelles.
CE851 First Arab recorded sighting of Seychelles.
1275 Marco Polo tells Kublai Khan of the (mythological) roc bird in the Indian Ocean.

1502 Amirantes islands named after Admiral Vasco da Gama, Portuguese navigator.
1609 First British landing. Recorded by John Jourdain.
1742 First French landing by Lazare Picault.
1756 Stone of Possession laid on Mahé. Islands named Séchelles; first settlement follows in 1770.
1814 Seychelles ceded to Britain.
1835 Abolition of slavery.
1862 Following torrential rains, 75 die in Victoria's Great Avalanche.

1903 Seychelles separates from Mauritius.
1971 Airport opened by the Queen; tourism soars.
29 June 1976 Independence from Britain. James Mancham becomes President.
5 June 1977 Prime Minister Albert René's coup d'état.
1993 First multiparty elections.
2006 Opposition Leader Anglican priest Wavel Ramkalawan contests presidential election.
2005 onwards Arab Russian land/hotel investment.

rugby team, guns hidden under toys. They were stopped at the airport and later, in typically generous Seychelles fashion, pardoned. In a bid to end the paranoia about invasions and intrigue, René stepped up his rhetoric against the exiled 'Movement for the Resistance', which was dealt a mortal blow in 1985 when its talented young leader Gerard Hoarau fell to a mysterious assassin's bullet in a London street.

Political instability is never good for tourism. The economy started to sour, and some of René's lieutenants abandoned him. The influential Catholic Church intensified its criticism, and pressure mounted for a return to free elections. Wily as ever (touched, perhaps by De Quincy's spirit), René suddenly reversed direction and agreed to an election in 1993, only to knock the wind out of everyone's sails by winning 60% of the vote, and so retaining the Presidency.

Opposition was at least now legal, journalistic criticism allowed, and Mancham was back in Seychelles as leader of the opposition Democratic Party. René retired in 2004, albeit as a benevolent *eminence grise,* and was replaced by his former vice president James Michel. His new People's Party won 55% of the vote at the 2011 general election.

GETTING AHEAD

Seychelles is almost totally literate, with doctors, computer buffs, engineers, aircraft pilots, businessmen and teachers. Nearly one-third of the population is under 18 and there are 9500 pupils in primary school and 8000 in secondary. There is a school for gifted children, a polytechnic and embryonic university offering business studies and engineering, and a hotel training school. The Seychellois nearly all speak English and French, and many speak Italian and German as well.

GOVERNMENT AND ECONOMY

Albert René's long if at times authoritarian rule as President (1977–2004) transformed Seychelles from an impoverished coconut colony a thousand miles from anywhere to an island country in which practically everyone has a job, a pension, access to free education, health facilities, and a government loan to build a home – benevolent and successful New Age socialism. But the old order changes, new wants emerge and René read the signs well. Free speech, press and elections are turning Seychelles into a tentative democracy.

▼ *Below: Air Seychelles' De Havilland Twin Otters hop between many of the archipelago's islands.*

INTRODUCING SEYCHELLES

Kathy Mason was the first tour operator in Seychelles. She started with a hole-in-the-wall office, taking groups in a small boat to Cerf Island for Sunday picnics, a family tradition. Innovative, dynamic and vivacious, she soon cornered much of the tourism business that increasingly came to Seychelles after the airport was constructed in 1971. Today, she, her husband Mickey, an equally adventurous ecological island farming entrepreneur, and university graduate son Alan run a stable that includes busy Mason's Travel, an inter-island ferry service, glass-bottom reef boats, the much sought-after Indian Ocean Lodge on Praslin and their own fabulous Denis Island. They employ some 400 people and run a fleet of 100 vehicles.

Economy

In pre-airport days of barefoot coconut collecting, colonial grants-in-aid, cinnamon, vanilla, and subsistence fishing, the average Seychellois was dirt poor. But tourism, tuna canning, construction and aggressive social planning have said goodbye to all that. Fully 40% of the population is employed, the average GDP per capita (2010) was US$10,788, the minimum wage per month US$582, far higher than that of their African neighbours, and everyone has a house, clean water, TV, telephone and many, a car. Over 9000 children attend secondary schools and the literacy rate is 94%. But this comes at a price: a large and continuous balance of trade deficit. Fuel accounts for 25% of imports and foodstuffs another 25%. Seychelles is suffering from its ambitious – if understandable – social agenda, a lack perhaps of Seychellois shareholding in its large forex-exporting hotels and a lingering attachment to a centrally controlled economy.

Seychelles, forex-hungry (import costs are double export's), is rather hurriedly selling land and islands to oil-rich Sheiks, Russians, Mauritians and South Africans – own a piece of Seychelles, they advertise. This, together with indentured Asian labour and a near total reliance on imported goods, could prove to be two-edged.

A Holiday Package

Once upon a time, the British Indian Steam Navigation liners would call monthly in Seychelles, and the occasional British warship would appear, show a film on Gordon Square (now Freedom Square) and play a football match against the local team. Until the airport was built in 1971 the Seychelles were the forgotten islands.

While the coming of tourism has exposed the Seychellois to prying cameras, consumer brand names, topless bathers and foreigners tramping through their Eden, the money is good and with few natural resources other than its beauty, its tuna canning and its people, it was always going to be one of the few industries Seychelles could exploit on any realistic economic

◄ Left: Relaxing in front of the idyllic Indian Ocean Lodge, Praslin.

scale. Apart from the jitteriness of an ever-fickle market, the 2008 worldwide recession, sudden 34% inflation and the uncertainty of the euro, the islands have done a remarkably good job, and high-end tourism sits squarely as the cornerstone of Seychelles' economy.

In the need to attract investment and create employment, Seychelles is financially caught between reef and rough surf. It has managed to retain control of some 30% of its visitor accommodation and these mainly small establishments. Of the 31 large hotels and coral island resorts, 75% are owned by foreign investors, mainly Maldivian, Malaysian, Mauritian, Arab, Russian and South African, resulting in high forex remittances. The coral island resorts, e.g. Denis Island and Bird, are by far the most appealing destinations. The large hotels, spas and resorts, some with a despoiling density of 400 rooms, are luxurious in a Brazilian *telenova* way but in spite of arrival champagne, wondrous foyers, and unbelievably stunning beaches they naturally lack the local charm and cuisine of the 95 family-run hotels and B&Bs that dot the islands. There are over 175,000 tourists annually, 75% from Europe and now Russia and the Arab states.

FAMOUS VISITORS

Noel Coward. Complained of fungus on his hotel wall.
Ian Fleming. Underwater scenes in *Thunderball*.
Ronald Reagan. Hollywood actor. Stayed on Praslin.
Archbishop Makarios. Climbed the mountains in flowing robes.
Pope John Paul II. Huge attendance at his Mass.
Tony Blair. He and his family visited twice.
Wilbur Smith. Pied-à-terre on Cerf Island.
Boney M. They and 180 guests flown in for a Russian wedding on Silhouette Island.
Prince William and Kate. They honeymooned in the Seychelles.
Pierce Brosnan and **Sir Paul McCartney**. Among many celebrities to visit Seychelles.

▼ *Below: These giant* omar *or* lobsters can be blue or green and are delicious.

Fishing

Surrounded by ocean and coral reef, fishing by handline, indigenous *kazye* trap and harpoon has always been Seychelles' primary harvest, diet and pastime. Some 4000 tonnes of fish are landed annually, while 400,000 tons of tuna caught by foreign vessels and trans-shipped in Mahé is, in an era of depleted tuna stocks, proving controversial. About 40,000 tonnes is canned locally accounting for 90% of Seychelles exports. The factory is sited near the Inter Island schooner and catamaran terminal and can be smelt from afar. Giant clams – the blessing fonts you see as you enter the older churches – prawns and black pearl oysters are also farmed for export.

Agriculture

To all those who dropped anchor in Seychelles' blue waters down the centuries, the islands were always regarded as a bountiful paradise. However, even Eden's natural resources suffered at the hands of those who came, as tortoises were curiosities, turtles a popular source of fresh meat and the tall trees highly valued as shipbuilding timber.

In general, the alkaline granite soil is not generous, and trying to grow anything on Seychelles for profit was at best a risky enterprise. Plantations of **copra**, **cinnamon**, **patchouli** and **vanilla** all enjoyed short-lived booms but the plantation owners or *grands blancs* seldom had the wherewithal to match their refined aspirations.

Seychellois are instinctive and innovative farmers. Everybody has a vegetable garden, fruit trees and where land is available, such as the carefully farmed Denis Island, there are chickens for export, fresh milk for the luxury lodge and honey for the table.

Tea from the slopes of Mahé's mountains supplies local requirement (try the *citronelle*). Seychelles is self-sufficient in chicken, beef, pigs and, for visitors' candle-lit dinners, orchids. There are substantial vegetable farms on all the larger islands.

Brisk Business

Manufacturing and business in Seychelles have flourished albeit in a small way. Many businesses, such as restaurants and craft shops, benefit from the considerable spin-offs from tourism, but there are also architects, lawyers, boat-builders, dressmakers and furniture-makers doing well. There is a daily paper and at least three weeklies, and a broadcasting company, Seychelles Broadcasting Cor-

▲ Above: Everyone has a breadfruit in their back yard, some larger than others.

poration. Being an island, shipping and tanker deliveries are prosperous concerns, while the presence of Cable and Wireless and their competitor Airtel has ensured an excellent and modern communication system. Seychelles appears in the *Guinness Book of Records* as being the smallest nation to run its own international airline.

Seychelles has offshore banking offering international trusts, mutual funds and ship registration. There are tax incentives for investors and a development bank for new projects. The conference centre in Victoria seats 600, a favourite with African states as Seychelles is considered safer.

Importing practically everything and being a touch casual about utilizing its own resources, Seychelles limits itself to producing beer, tea, tuna, black pearls and bottled spring water, while cigarettes, milk and fruit juices are reprocessed from imported stocks. Local plastic-packaged manioc and banana chips are marvellous. But other than oodles of palms, beaches and azure seas, there is nothing developing-world cheap about Seychelles. The recently instituted floating bank exchange rate is roughly SR12 to US$1, and the black market has disappeared. (For many years Seychelles quoted in Euros, but visitors no longer have to pay for services in forex.) Devaluation has hit local folk where it hurts. You won't find a McDonald's but a Seybrew costs US$5 in a hotel. The key remains whether tourism can be maintained to match the good life the Seychellois have come to accept as normal.

MARINE PARK ISLANDS

There are six islands in the Ste Anne Marine Park off Victoria: the pyramid-shaped **Ste Anne** (the largest), **Cerf** (everyone's favourite Sunday picnic island), **Round**, **Long**, **Moyenne** and **Cachee** (Hidden). There are six resorts, a special one being L'Habitation on Cerf. Noteworthy among the three independent restaurants is the quixotic Jolly Roger on Moyenne. There is one self-catering facility, the Fairy Tern. You can walk round Round Island in 15 minutes. Each island has its own distinctive flavour and exquisite off-shore corals.

SHADES OF SEYCHELLES

Colour hardly matters now in post-tourism boom Seychelles, although it used to. Someone of Indian descent was a *Malbar*, a very dark person a *Mazambik*, a European who had gone to seed a *blanc rouillé coco* (white rusting among the coconuts). There are no more *grands blancs* (quasi-aristocratic French planta-tion owners); they have quietly exchanged a drop in status for the lucrative egalitarianism of tourism.

THE PEOPLE

Western writers have always described the Seychellois as smiling, happy-go-lucky folk straight out of a Gauguin painting. Nonsense. The Seychellois certainly know and take advantage of the paradise in which they live, and the climate and beauty make them fairly laid-back, but they are not beaming, brown-skinned natives in sarongs singing love songs as the long boats ride in on the surf. They are canny, wily, island folk 'with one thousand virtues and a few hundred vices' as former President Mancham wrote in his poem. Drawn from African, Malagasy, Indian, Chinese, and European roots, they have developed a unique and adaptable culture with a great sense of fun and an irrepressible knack for gossiping – at every bus stop, street corner and shop.

The Seychellois can be welcoming, quick to offer help or to invite you home for a meal, and happy to share their knowledge of the islands. Tourism has changed their lives, but it has not trampled their spirit. At the least hint of arrogance or condescension they will freeze you out, but the welcome in hotels, initially a touch hesitant, is soon exuberant and tinged with humour.

▼ *Below: Tin shops perch precariously on the roadside at Quatre Bornes.*

Family Life

Coming out of the times when there were no priests, slaves were not allowed to marry (their children automatically belonged to the master) and in any event a wedding feast was prohibitive, a tradition of living *en ménage* (together) without marrying took root. Families tend to be rather loose arrangements. The many children 'born on the outside' are commonly looked after by their mother alone. **Seychellois women** are confident, shrewd, and often the fulcrum of society. There are proportionately more women in the Seychelles parliament than in any other country, and they are often the power behind many businesses.

▲ *Above: Colourful gear*, de rigueur *for basketball guys.*

Language

There is really no such thing as a Kreol person in Seychelles. 'Creoles' live in Louisiana. Everyone is Seychellois, and their language is **Kreol**, sometimes written 'Creole', based on the French of plantation days, but it has strong African intonations and has, over the years, incorporated a good many English words, Malagasy, Indian, Arabic, and more recently, truncated hip-hop speak. A French speaker will understand it, although to read it in its written form is mind-boggling.

USEFUL KREOL EXPRESSIONS

Knowing a few words of Kreol will always win you friends:
Good morning, sir • *bonzour msye* (pronounce it phonetically)
Where's the road, brother? • *Oli semen, mon frer?* (From old French: *Où est le chemin, mon frère?*)
Please, madam, what time does the bus get here? • *Pardon, madam, ou capab di mwa, keler bis yarive?* (Roughly from old French: *Pardon, madame, quand est-ce que arrive le bus ici?*)
May I use your toilet, please? • *Mwan kapab servi ou kabinen silvouple?*
Is there a shop over there? • *I annan en laboutik laba?*
I am going to … • *Mon pe al kot …*
Excuse me • *Eskiz mwan*
Yes, no • *wi, non*
Do you speak English, madam? • *Ou koz Angle, madam?*
Hotel • *lotel*
I don't know • *mon pa konnen*
How much? • *konbyen sa?*
One, two, three • *enn, de, twa*
And, everyone's favourite words in Kreol:
kouyon • expletive – used liberally to cover every volatile situation, self-recrimination and motoring confrontation.
Bouldou or *kwaver* • sweetheart or knee-trembler.

RADIO BANBOU

The BBC, CNN and the French RFI news bulletins are broadcast via the Seychelles Broadcasting Corporation while Paradise FM vibrates with Kreolised Julian Marley, sega and pop at Sunday beach picnics. TV includes dubbed Brazilian soaps – will the Sheikh of Abu Dhabi give us solar panels for allowing his master palace to be built? But *Radio Banbou* (or radio bamboo) gossip really ignites the ether. Marketplace, hotel reception or bus station. Did that Russian Mafioso buy a Seychelles passport? Are La Digueois women so plentiful that you can *kas dan pye, met dan pos* – break them off the coconut trees and tuck them in your pocket?

Kreol is also spoken in Mauritius and in parts of the Caribbean, but Seychelles was the first country to develop it as a written medium and give it equal status as an official language. It is a living, changing language, and a Kreol Institute has been set up in Mahé to promote it. Primary school children used to be taught in Kreol although this has changed to English. Business and law use English, those of French descent speak that language at home, and the news is read on television in all three.

Religion

The **Catholic** faith, to which 89% of the population are adherents, remains at the core of Seychellois culture. The menfolk, except at funerals, affect to treat that bond lightly, but there is no doubting the strength of it, and one of the images of the islands is the colourfully dressed worshippers on their way to Sunday Mass – men in starched white shirts, the older ladies with hats, and the young girls in their lovingly sewn first communion dresses.

Inside church, with the scent of eau de cologne and coconut cream wafting under the fans, the atmosphere is heady. The singing is excellent, especially at churches served by the increasing number of young Seychellois priests, while features such as the marquetry interior of Our Lady of Seven Sorrows at Anse Boileau and the impressive altar windows of the rebuilt Anglican cathedral in Victoria lift the spirit.

There are beautiful grottoes along every remote road in Seychelles, and the church bell tower is the focal point of each tiny village. Many islanders still cross themselves passing a church, even if they're in a bus. Saints' feast days are grand events, especially La Digue's *fête* on 15 August, with bunting, sports competitions, feasting, music and processions.

Other religions and denominations do have a presence. There are four Anglican churches in Seychelles; in Victoria there is a new Hindu temple and a mosque; and there are also smart Jehovah's Witness, Seventh Day Adventist and a 700-seater Pentecostal Assembly Church. In the days before electricity there was substantial belief in *gris gris* (black magic), but with a young modern population it mainly exists today as effective herbalism, folk memory and party banter.

◀ *Opposite: Every faith flourishes in Seychelles, such as Baha'í near the schooner quay in Praslin.*
▼ *Below: A wayside shrine on a country road bears witness to the islands' Roman Catholic heritage.*

INTRODUCING SEYCHELLES

MUSIC MAN

Patrick Victor is a big dark man with a rose in his hat and sorrow in his eyes. Post independence he did much to rescue Seychelles folk music from extinction, especially the *moutya* music of the mountains and the poor. He grew up the eldest of nine children near the Nageeon plantation in the country village of Pointe La Rue, which is now buried under the airport. His mission was 'to put the soul of the past into the present', and in doing so he has played all over Europe and Africa. Today he faces competition from David André, Antoinette Dodin and Dave Sinon.

Music and Dance

There are travel, coffee-table, historical, diving and guidebooks galore on Seychelles. But apart from the mischievous Soungoula stories, Glynn Burridge's *Voices* and Paul Tingay's novels, there is very little literature. The lush tropical atmosphere of Seychelles has always been an inspiration for artists, but it is music that truly captures the spirit of the islands, and no more so than the defiant, evocative *moutya*. High in the mountains or on a remote beach a slow chanting and sensuous shuffle dance would begin around a fire made from dry coconut fronds, a line of men facing another of women, everyone else watching. Born in slave days, the *moutya* is pure Africa, the rumbling drum evoking anguished memories of another time. It was frowned upon by the establishment, who were seldom invited to the all-night rave-ups, and naughty children would get a hiding from parents for sneaking a peak. These days, to save milady's blushes, visitors are treated to a considerably refined version at hotel dinners and folk festivals.

The sega comes from the Sri Lankan *Baila*, the playing of which is no longer allowed in buses (together with loud talking, the notice reads). It is danced in colourful Mauritian costumes. The islanders' (and some would say more wicked) version is danced with small, rhythmic steps and a much subtler sway in the hips, neither partner ever touching.

Family dances and weddings are jolly affairs, with violins, banjo, accordion, triangle and drums providing the music for *kamtole* – Seychelles waltzes, polkas, masok and contredanse, performed with shouted instructions from a *komander*, rather like country and western.

▼ *Below: Sega dancing – sensual, striking, and straight from the deeply rooted Kreol tradition.*

Leading musicians in Seychelles include Patrick Victor, a *moutya* poet and folk singer, classically trained David André (his *nostalgie* music with Xu Lu's violin is exquisite), Jenny Letourdi, Antoinette Dodin *(Perdi maman, perdi tou)* and you must not leave Seychelles without seeing the dancing and music of Kevin Valentin Sokwe's *moutya* and sega group. Sophisticated, sensual, superb.

No-one, however, has reached the standing of old folk hero Tonpa, legendary master of the Seychelles *bonm* (bow and gourd). Above the fountain at La Bastille Archives in Victoria there is a bust of Tonpa and two friends on the *zez*, *bonm* and *tambour* (drum), playing, as Victor's *moutya* song goes, '…until dawn breaks, and it's time to milk the goats'.

Island Cuisine

With a heritage drawing from French, Indian, Chinese and Kreol roots, the quality of the cuisine in Seychelles could only be wonderful. Few menus fail to be mouthwatering. The staples of the Seychellois diet are *kordonnyen* fish, rice, coconut, breadfruit, chillies, spices and mangoes, each of them cooked in a hundred different and delicious ways. Indian dal or yellow lentils are commonly made into a thick soup, while saffron rice is served with an onion, orange and spices salad as a picnic pilau with grilled suckling pig. Various types of seafood are always popular, among them grilled *bourzwa* snapper fish, cold *zob* fish, and fresh *tectec* clams – dug up from the beach, and then made into a soup. Other delicacies of the islands are *satini rekin* (dried shark chutney), smoked sailfish and fruit bat, but perhaps nothing beats the simplest rice and salted fish in a banana frond pouch, fisherman style.

NATURAL RHYTHMS

The traditional musical instruments of Seychelles are made from various local materials. These include:
- an old tin or calabash as a sounding box in both the *zez* and *bonm*.
- a bamboo cone and strings from bamboo bark used to make a *mouloumba*, a cross between a megaphone and a violin.
- the *tamtam* is a hollowed-out tree trunk. The *tambour* is made from a roundel of *Karambol* wood. A manta ray or goat skin is then stretched over this and heated to maximize resonance.

▼ *Below: Karang is a good catch and delicious.*

▶ Right: *Island cuisine is often decorated with exquisite flowers.*
▶▶ *Opposite: Thrills and paragliding spills at Beau Vallon beach.*

THE BREADFRUIT TREE

The story has it that if you eat breadfruit in Seychelles you'll always come back. These dark green trees grow all over Seychelles. The leaves are rather like giant oak leaves, and the green cannonball fruit make great eating. When ripe they weigh in at 3kg (7 lb) and fall in a yellow mush to the ground; cut them down with a long stick and catch them (if you're clever) before they fall and serve as chips, mashed, or made into a pudding with coconut milk. Best of all, eat them baked whole over an open coconut husk fire. It is supposed to be the Tree of Life and everyone has a tree in their garden. The texture is bread-like, though it is not made into bread. 'A poor substitute for potatoes', one writer in 1940 sniffed. The wood from the tree makes good floor planking.

For dessert, go for bananas fried in brown sugar or pineapple in red wine. A few of the other delights are manioc (cassava) as a pudding cooked in freshly grated coconut, sweet potatoes in honey, or wild *framboises* from the mountains of La Misère. Sweets are made of *pample-mousse* peel, jams from *zamalak* fruit, and popular snacks are *gato pimen* chillibites and nougat coco. The local beers are pretty ordinary. Wines are super expensive. Try *kalou* (coconut tree toddy), or, for a real blast, *bacca* rum. Lemon grass or *citronelle* tea helps the digestion. There are a number of excellent restaurants around the islands, but, if the opportunity arises, never turn up the chance of home cooking.

Sport and Recreation

People tend to wake up with the six o'clock sun, so wild all-hours revelling is not common, though hotels with their discos, casinos, coffee shops and barbecues have replaced much of the home entertainment, which is usually folksy accordion singsongs and dancing. After church on Sunday, the done thing is a crate of Seybrew, ghetto blaster and giggle with the gals picnic to Port Launay or Anse La Mouche beaches.

Sitting on an upturned bucket in a village back yard to the ferocious slapping of dominoes is a regular rite all through the islands. It is universally addictive among men, along with football (35 teams) and athletics (long jump), the two main sports in which Seychelles competes, with distinction, internationally. Diving, swimming, running, weight lifting and an annual 40km (25-mile) windsurfing race to Praslin are also popular with many.

In Seychelles everyone is a fisherman, and making friends with the *pêcheur* nearest to your particular beach could avoid the cost of big sea charters. Golf is played at the Reef golf course – where the hazards include falling coconuts and crabs with a reputation for stealing balls – and at Lémuria resort on Praslin. You can also ride horses at Barbarons and La Digue, paraglide or jetski noisily at Beau Vallon, and find all the regular water sports at most big hotels.

2
North Mahé

Mahé is the largest of the widely spread islands of Seychelles, only 27km (17 miles) long but given an impressive presence by a backbone of high forested mountains. These granitic peaks are the highest in the archipelago, and a distinguishing feature since they were first sighted by Arab seamen. Mahé was the site of the first French landings in 1742, and the first settlement in 1770. Today 87% of the population of Seychelles lives on the island, with a large proportion of that figure in the nation's capital, **Victoria** (population 26,000).

Around Mahé's coastline there are 75 beaches and coves (known as 'anse' in Seychelles), ranging from long, sweeping stretches of sand to isolated little bays tucked among granite cliffs and thick green trees. Except for the western corner, a narrow and twisting tarred road rings the island; it fringes sea, reef and an overgrown coconut jungle dotted with green- and red-tiled homes and precariously perched general stores.

The side of Mahé to the northeast of the central range of mountains encompasses the three most important single locations on the island: the **airport** at Point La Rue, the capital, Victoria, and **Beau Vallon Bay**, the principal tourist area. Victoria is the main harbour in Seychelles, and the heart of business and commerce. It rises quickly into the mountains, through leafy suburbs such as Bel Air and Bel Eau. Driving north, the land soon becomes more rural, albeit fringed by land reclamation islands and their ubiquitous

CLIMATE

The sea and winds keep Mahé refreshed. **Humidity** is around 80% all year. To some extent, the buildings and paved roads of Victoria hold in the heat and make it hotter than the rural and mountain areas.
Temperature is 29ºC (84ºF) year-round, with only a slight drop at night. **Rain** falls heavily from November to March but drops to as low as 50mm (2 in) in July.

◄ *Opposite: A stormy rainbow on Le Niol heights overlooking Beau Vallon.*

DON'T MISS

*** **Beau Vallon Beach:** the definitive Seychelles beach, 15 minutes from Victoria.
*** **Victoria Walkabout:** start at the Clock Tower, and take in all the sights, sounds and smells of the capital.
*** **Ste Anne Marine National Park:** just off Victoria, a feast of coral and fish. See it from the comfort of a glass semi-submersible.
** **Botanical Gardens:** a downtown taste of the spectacular Seychelles flora, coco de mer, tortoises and lunch.
** **The Market:** everything exotic for sale and some great personalities.
** **Game Fishing:** boats from Marine Charter next to the yacht club.
* **Natural History Museum:** near Clock Tower; 43 original Marianne North paintings. And crocodile skulls.
* **National Library, Historical Museum and Art Gallery:** near Le Chantier fountain roundabout.

casuarinas. The first whispering palms and rumbling reef are at North East Point. Mahé's top beach, Beau Vallon, is only a 15-minute drive over the mountain saddle from Victoria, while huddled in the wide bay of the eastern coastline are a group of small islands that are incorporated in **Ste Anne Marine National Park**, a kaleidoscopic if threatened garden of underwater life.

VICTORIA

From the air or the sea Victoria seems to be lost in a green jungle beneath the towering black cliffs of Trois Frères. The first French inhabitants were attracted to the sheltered anchorage, but the land must have seemed an impenetrable swathe of mangrove swamp. The settlement was initially called L'Etablissement, before becoming Victoria in 1841 in honour of the Queen. It is the seat of government, the location of most of the main institutions and businesses, and the only centre in the 115 islands that can really be described as a town.

Victoria's size has been substantially increased in recent years by land reclamation, which has allowed the development of the New Port, the airport, a large tuna cannery, a sports complex, new factories, and clusters of high-density flats. The new double highway to the airport enables cars to reach 80kph (50mph). Still, it is one of the smallest capitals in the world – you can stroll

from one end of town to the other in 20 minutes. Buses and pedestrians dodge and weave through the town's narrow streets. Colourful, corrugated iron chateaux with drooping balconies stand defiantly beside chunky modern buildings, while along the tree-lined pavements life bustles with street stalls, music and closely packed general stores.

A Walk around the Clock ★★★

Victoria is small enough that it doesn't take long to see everything on foot. You quickly pick up the chirpiness of the Seychellois and the relaxed tropical feel of the place. The focal point of town is the **Clock Tower**, erected in 1903 to mark Seychelles' coming of age as a separate colony. Before land reclamation it marked the old harbour shore. During the 2004 tsunami, waters swept up to the base of the clock. One wag reckoned he even saw a shark.

Starting at the Clock Tower, set off along Francis Rachel – it was named after one of the insurgents killed during the coup d'état 30 years ago. An avenue of shady trees and flowers runs past the gracious 1887 courthouse opposite Temooljies with its bust of Pierre Poivre (Peter Pepper) who in 1772 introduced cinnamon to Seychelles. Some of the remaining old timber and tin-roofed shops are still there: Adam Moosa, Chaka Brothers. These are food, cloth and hardware merchants which date back to colonial days when they were the islands' bankers, offering 'indefinite credit and unfailing courtesy'. Their sons and grandsons still greet you with old-world politesse as you enter, even if you can no longer buy a bottle of homemade lemonade with a marble stopper. The local crafts kiosks, formerly enlivening the clock tower, are now beneath the trees of Fiennes Esplanade.

▲ *Above: The Victorian Clock Tower, in memory of Her Majesty, 'Empress of India'.*
◄ *Opposite: Beyond Victoria harbour, reclaimed islands much loved by developers have been created.*

The ultramodern facilities of Cable and Wireless are alongside the old grey and white colonial façade of **Kenwyn House**, a national monument. Nearby is the **Mosque** of Sheik Mohamed bin Khalifa. Carry on past the **National Library**, **Historical Museum**, **Archives and Art Gallery** with its Grecian columns and you come to the huge dark trees marking **Le Chantier** fountain and roundabout, site of the old boat-building yard and today gateway to **New Port** and the airport road.

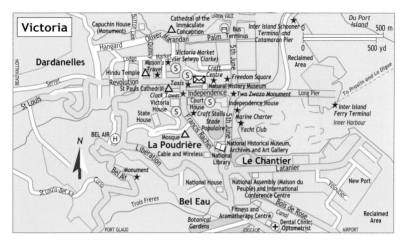

**WHERE THE CLOCK
CHIMES TWICE**

There is a clock that chimes in Victoria, but it isn't the Clock Tower in the middle of town. A crucial part was lost over the side of the ship as the commemorative clock was unloaded in 1903, and no-one could make the bell work after that. What you will hear chiming is the clock in the Roman Catholic Cathedral, beyond the market. When the travel writer Alec Waugh (brother of the novelist Evelyn) came to Seychelles, he wrote a book called *Where the Clock Chimes Twice*. And why does it chime twice? One version is that the first is to wake everyone up, and the second to tell them the time.

Opposite, along Latanier Road, is the **National Assembly**, or *Maison du Peuple,* and **International Conference Centre**, partly hidden by trees, and beyond it the power station and port office. Continue the walk by doubling back along 5th June Avenue (the day of the coup in 1977, Liberation Day) towards the town centre, passing a children's playground, then the **yacht club**, with halyards clattering in the breeze, and the **Marine Charter quay**. The de-shackling of Rousseau-like chains marks the rather enthusiastically executed **Zom Libre Independence statue** across the road.

A left turn at the roundabout of three soaring mod-art fairy terns, a statue known locally as Twa Zwazo, defines the start of Independence Avenue which will take you past the helpful **Tourist Office** in Independence House, and then back past two photo shops (Kim Koon and Photo Eden) and Pirates Arms (hard-drinking planters and Colonial servants always drank here or at the long gone **Seychelles Club**) to the Clock Tower, while the Long Pier road behind you leads to the fishing port, tuna cannery and finally the inter-island schooner, helistop and seacat terminal. While busy schooners load cargo, you look out across the Cerf Passage, often with large tuna fishing boats anchored in it, to the string of islands in Ste Anne Marine National Park. The old B.I. ships of yesteryear used to anchor out in the roads, where in earlier days young men would dive 18m (60ft) to the sea bed to retrieve thrown coins.

Natural History Museum ★

The tiny Natural History Museum next door to the post office, and once the venerable Carnegie Library, is one of the few old wide-staircase buildings that has survived. Seychelles has 1000 marine fish species, 450 species of molluscs, 100 different types of hard corals, nine different types of breeding terns, giant tortoises, freshwater terrapins and turtles. The wolf snake is the most distinctive of Seychelles' three non-poisonous types. Tiny sooglossid frogs hide up the mountains, lizards hang from walls and bright green geckos on trees. The 700 beetle types include the endemic giant tenebrionid beetle. There are 766 species of flowering plants and 85 ferns on the granitic islands, and 350 types of seaweed. The pride of Seychelles is the coco de mer. You can learn about all this biodiversity by strolling around the museum's cabinets and displays. Upstairs are Marianne North's 43 magnificent flower and plant paintings of Seychelles 120 years ago. (Open Monday–Friday and Saturday mornings.)

National Library, Historical Museum, Archives and Art Gallery ★

Built by public subscription, the three-storey National Library belongs to a school of architecture which can only be described as tropic gothic – Grecian columns and soaring space. There are permanent exhibitions on slavery and the British colonial rule that ended it. Look out for pirates' pistols, old Seychellois musical instruments, Mahé in Victorian

▼ *Below: The elegant National Library and Historical Museum.*

days, shipwrecks, pictures of British Governors and the 1841 bust of Queen Victoria (supposedly the world's smallest) which used to grace the drinking fountain outside the Courthouse. Even more fascinating is the 1756 Possession Stone, the symbol of French claim to the islands, and another, an old pirate's tombstone inscribed, with skull and crossbones, which reads: 'Jean-Pierre Le Chartier, killed on March 4, 1805 by his friend Evellon. Passers-by pray for me'. Whether for pirate or his murderer is left unsaid.

Inside, it is lovely. There are not a great many books, but it has an unhurried reference department, and it is a wonderful home for Seychelles art. The building is also home to the Legislative Assembly.

Shopping

The craft kiosks along Fiennes Esplanade sell local shopping bags, beach wraps, hats of coconut fibre, postcards and souvenirs. Avoid the pretty seashells. They look better untouched, underwater. 'Tortoiseshell' items made from the shell of hawksbill turtles was a fine art in Seychelles years ago. Now it is forbidden. Near the Clock Tower is Lakaz Cooperative selling local crafts and in the Pirates Arms arcade, Antik

Colony. The Post Office has a philatelic bureau.

There is a good bookshop, Antigone, maps at the Survey Office and, still in Independence Avenue, airline offices and photo shops. Past the new Anglican Cathedral you come to Camion Hall (after the *camions* or trucks, Seychelles' first buses that parked here as did long gone rickshas). The arcade shops include a Duty Free, Kreol d'Or's gold and local black oyster pearl jewellery, and opticians *Ou Linet* (your specs). There are at least five Internet cafés, 13 estate agents, flower shops, and seven banks (ATMs). Also in Albert Street is the Sooty Tern, selling works of three local artists. The SMB Supermarket is not Waitrose. In pre-revolutionary days it belonged to President Mancham's family. The Manchams today own a new bookstore, Victoria, just around the corner opposite the police station.

▲ *Above: Sunshine or rain, there is always something interesting to buy at Victoria's market.*
◄ *Opposite: The Clock Tower (rare 1939 painting by Emile Hugon).*

In Revolution Avenue, where the terrible avalanche of 1862 swept down, is the police station opposite Mason's Travel, the first tour operator in Seychelles.

Market Street, a pedestrian mall, is the shopping hub for Seychelles housewives. The little shops sell everything from local music to video cameras. Kanti, an expert on Seychelles, always appreciates a chat in his rickety tin-roofed shop, Jivan's. If you're beautiful and female, Kanti (89) will read your palm.

Victoria Market ★★

The action-packed market is hard to miss under its elegant new roof and courtyard mango trees in Market Street. Started in 1839, it is still called the Sir Selwyn-Clarke Market after the medical doctor and post-World War II Governor. It is open every day except Sunday, with Saturday being particularly hectic. The best time to be there is when the fish are heaved in.

The market is a hive of all things strange and exotic. You can buy *bourzwa* red snapper heads for soup, pale green chilli-like *sousout*, or *patole* (a sort of hollow cucumber), *zamalak* fruits, mangoes (ripe or unripe), *fatak* reed brooms, coconut graters, and chillies, the smaller the hotter.

BEST BUYS

- **Baskets, bags and hats.** Palm weave.
- **Black oyster pearls.** From Praslin.
- **Gold jewellery** weaved into local cowries, coconut shell and mother-of-pearl.
- *Moutya* **CDs.** Patrick Victor, Jany Letourdie, David André, Jean Marc Volcy.
- **Island paintings.** A dozen artists. Superb.
- **Spices.** *Karambol* jam and honey. Mr Lolo Joseph Adrienne in the market.
- **Takamaka Bay rum.** *Grandpère* D'Offay's secret recipe.
- **Perfumes.** Kreolfleurage from local spices and exotic flowers.

▶ Opposite: The colonial elegance of State House and its ancient trees and designer gardens.

The best part of the market, however, is near the back where some wonderful characters keep their stalls. Look out for diminutive Joseph Lolo Adrienne's bottled jams and chutneys. He will explain with all the tricks and treats of a medicine man how to cook with his special curry powders and hellfire sauces. Or try speaking a few words of Kreol to Yvonne Sidoney at her fruit, vegetable and *gallette mayok* (a crusty biscuit made of manioc) stall, and you'll make a lifelong friend. Shoo away the white egrets, which are called *Madam Paton* by the locals (after a white-haired lady who bore a resemblance), as you taste some of the wonderful delicacies.

The Botanical Gardens ★★

Industrial wealth, a far-flung empire and botanist Charles Darwin's studies on evolution caused an explosion of interest in birds and bees in Victorian Britain. One outcome was Kew Gardens in London; another – if not quite so grand – was the Botanical Gardens in Seychelles.

The entrance to the Botanical Gardens is less than a mile south of town parallel with the road leading up to the hospital. Coco de mer palms dominate the path up into the Gardens. Others of the islands' six endemic palms to be found there include *latanier*, which is used for thatching, and *palmiste*, the favourite ingredient for millionaire's salad.

The Gardens lie in a granite-humped, grassy strip between two small streams trickling down from the massif that soars above the trees. Water lilies, papyrus, and even some tiny fish and transparent shrimps can be spotted here. The 6ha (15-acre) Gardens were established over 100 years ago and owe a lot to their original Director, Paul Rivaltz Dupont, who travelled the world gathering exotic trees and plants. Many of the unusual trees are labelled. There is a nursery for young plants, an orchid garden with samples of these exotic blooms from all over the world, a Seychelles giant tortoise pen formed by natural black boulders, and a thatched café,

Le Sapin, set like its namesake beneath Norfolk pines. Up the hill you might find fruit bats hanging upside down from the trees. There are over 30 palm types in the Gardens, and some 70 tree species including jackfruit, pink-flowered cannonball, teak and nutmeg, the seeds of which schoolboys heat by rubbing them against granite and then apply to unsuspecting chums' legs. The Gardens (entrance fee, open daily) are the Headquarters of Seychelles National Parks.

Cemetery

Three kilometres (2 miles) from town along the road to the south is Seychelles' main cemetery. Cemeteries may not be a common choice for a stroll, but this one has such an attractive swathe of bumpy grass, black granite and open mountain scenery that it deserves being the exception. Turn uphill in Mont Fleuri just before the old white coral wall and park. If it is near All Saints' Day (1 November) you'll see brightly coloured flowers on the black granite tombstones, time-worn mausoleums and newly whitewashed crosses that drift up the hill and to the mountains above you.

The inscriptions on the tombstones are often in French – the language always reserved for formal

> ### STATE HOUSE
>
> Completed in 1913, this gracious residence of colonial governors and presidents is sited on a small rise just above town. The house and manicured lawns were designed by Lady William Davidson, the wife of one of the governors. She neglected to include in her design a staircase for the two-storeyed house, a fact that was only discovered mid-construction. It has lofty white columns, two-storey high ceilings, polished floors, discreet staff and split cane roll-down blinds on the verandah where in colonial days *punkah-wallah* wafted luncheons would be held for those who signed the Visitors' Book. Access is by permission only. Queau de Quincy's tomb is in the grounds.

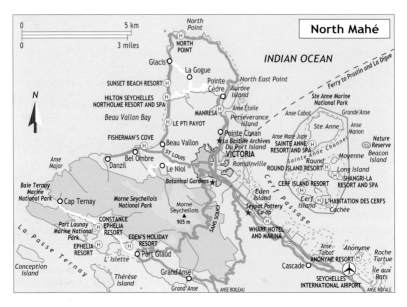

North Mahé

0 ____ 5 km
0 ____ 3 miles

North Point

NORTH POINT

INDIAN OCEAN

Ferry to Praslin and La Digue

Glacis
La Gogue
Pointe Cèdre
North East Point
Aurore Island
SUNSET BEACH RESORT (H)
Ste Anne Marine National Park
HILTON SEYCHELLES NORTHOLME RESORT AND SPA (H)
Anse Étoile
Grande'Anse
MANRESA
Perseverance Island
Anse Cabot
Beau Vallon Bay
(H) LE PTI PAYOT
Ste Anne
Anse Manon
FISHERMAN'S COVE
Pointe Conan
Anse Maré Jupe
Nature Reserve
(H) Beau Vallon
La Bastille Archives Du Port Island
SAINTE ANNE (H) RESORT AND SPA
Beacon Island
Anse Major
Bel Ombre
ST LOUIS
VICTORIA
Sainte Anne Channel
Moyenne
Danzil
Le Niol
Romainville
ROUND ISLAND RESORT
Round Island
Long Island
Botanical Gardens
CERF ISLAND RESORT
SHANGRI-LA RESORT AND SPA
Baie Ternay Marine National Park
Eden Island
Cerf Island
(H)
(H) L'HABITATION DES CERFS
Cap Ternay
Morne Seychelles National Park
Morne Seychellois
Seypot Pottery
Co-op
Cachée
CONSTANCE EPHELIA RESORT
Morne Seychellois 905 m
WHARF HOTEL AND MARINA
Port Launay Marine National Park
EDEN'S HOLIDAY RESORT
EPHELIA RESORT
L' Islette
Port Glaud
Anse Talbot
ANONYME RESORT (H)
Anonyme
Roche Tortue
Île aux Rats
Conception Island
Thérèse Island
Grand'Anse
Cascade
SEYCHELLES INTERNATIONAL AIRPORT
Grand'Anse
ANSE BOILEAU
ANSE ROYALE

La Passe Ternay

Sans Souci

Cerf Passage

N

In the 19th century (and perhaps a touch today) there was *Ti-Albert* voodoo herbalism, *dandotia* zombies (who will call if you sweep your yard after sunset), spells, chicken bones under pillows and tarot cards cast by the *bonhomme de bois*, the old fellow of the woods. *Gris gris* magic (if a *katiti*, or kestrel, roosts in your roof someone is going to die) adds that spicy touch for visitors and Seychelles is only too happy to exploit this attraction. They'll even produce a *nam* (ghost) for you in the old settlers' graveyard above Victoria where a 2.7m (9ft) 'giant' walks around his tomb. It was last seen by a tourist. Naturally.

occasions – but Kreol is found too on the little white home-made crosses.

From the road at the top of the cemetery there is a scenic walk back to town. It runs past Rochon, where women used to wash clothes in the river, slapping them against boulders and holding raucous conversations across from one level to the next. Under a tangled spaghetti of electricity and telephone wires, festooned with the webs of giant black and brown golden orb spiders, mynah birds yabber away as noisily as Paradise FM. A narrow footbridge beneath a dark canopy of trees crosses into the aptly named Forêt Noire (Black Forest). Not far beyond the forest there are views of the emerald waters of the harbour, with boats milling around the dock, and Ste Anne's Island beyond.

To complete the walk, cut left up Liberation Road just before National House to Bel Eau which seems steep until you come to another grand vista of the town. From here it is no more than a 15-minute walk back into town.

AROUND VICTORIA
Coastal Road South

A double highway damaged in the 2004 tsunami is the quickest route south from Victoria. But the old main road still twists past greenery, houses, tuck shops, brewery, reclaimed islands and lagoons. Tata buses thunder past, but a pleasant option is to walk it.

After the cemetery at **Mont Fleuri** you'll come to the **La Misère** mountain pass roundabout. Staying on the coast road you pass the church of **St Thérèse**, **Gerard Devoud's art gallery**, the **Seypot Pottery co-op**, the derelict schooner (and former restaurant) *Isle of Farquhar*, and then the bridge across the small **Mamelles River**. This used to mark the beginning of town, the start of dim streetlights and tarred road where you put on your shoes for the big city. It is also the site of the oldest plantation house in the islands, the elegant **Chateau des Mamelles**. Built in 1804, and formerly the residence of 'Le Corsair' Jean François Hodoul, it is now a national monument.

Past the busy Seychelles **brewery** is **Souverains des Mers**, where there is an exhibition of 40 model ships.

▼ *Below:* Twa Zwazo, *or Three Birds Monument, symbolizes the fusion of Africa, Europe and Asia in the Seychelles people.*

▼ Below: The area around Cascade's old church was badly damaged in the 2004 Indian Ocean tsunami.

Cascade

The alternative route from Victoria is along the new **Bois de Rose Avenue**, past the Roche Caiman housing estate which is not exactly blessed with architectural eloquence. But there is a lovely little bird sanctuary nearby. The elegant Wharf Marina's penthouse and moored cruisers give solace to gilded yachties. The afternoon wind whips the waves while across the road, small *katyolos* lie at anchor in the serpentine lagoon that borders the garden walls. Hardwoods are being planted along this road – which rapidly becomes Seychelles' only double highway – to supercede the forest of casuarinas that bond the coral rubble landfill.

Find a spot to get off the road and there are lovely views of mountain and mangrove shore. Watch for fiddler crabs at low tide. Red-steepled Cascade Church with its crumbling water mill, waterfall and pool is clearly visible not far from the double highway bridge swept away by the 2004 tsunami. In the old days Cascade was the choice mackerel fishing venue. Today you can almost touch an Air Seychelles Boeing 787 Dreamliner as it roars in to touch down at the airport on reclaimed land just ahead.

The elegant 1882 church (built originally as a wooden chapel) dominates Cascade water village and its precipitous lagoon-flanking causeway, the old road.

Northern Peninsula

The road north from Victoria winds past **Radio Seychelles**, **La Bastille National Archives**, and the now closed **Christian Broadcasting Station** (FEBA) with its red and white aerials marching out to sea, reaching **Anse Etoile**. During World War II British troops were quartered

◀ *Left: Massed granite stolidity on the shore of the northern peninsula.*

here, and although a bunker still juts defiantly out to sea, the Nazi submarines never came. Part of the bay was nicknamed 'smelly corner' after a U-shaped cove was filled in with refuse; it is now fully reclaimed.

Following the road around this northerly peninsula of Mahé the whole central massif is visible, with palm-fringed views back to Victoria, the brooding **Trois Frères** mountain range, the busy port, and across the bay to the coral reefs around Ste Anne's Island.

The reef at **North East Point** is closer to the shore than at any other beach in Seychelles. If you want to take a closer look, wear a pair of shoes and explore it at low tide. Otherwise take a stroll along the shell-strewn beach with its fringe of palms and casuarinas. The bay is not particularly good for swimming, but there is a lovely wildness about the area, exposed as it is to the ocean and both seasons' monsoon winds.

There is an alternate narrow metal drive, up through forest and breadfruits then down past the cemetery to link up with the main circular road at the 1882 Church of St John the Baptist at Glacis on the western side of the island. The road begins directly opposite Manresa Restaurant in Anse Etoile, a great place to have lunch. The route is named after Seychelles' main reservoir, La Gogue, unfortunately not accessible to the public. There are two little villages in the hills, **Maldive** and **La Gogue**, each with a cluster of breadfruit, mango and palm trees.

BEAUTY AND THE BEACH

- Best swimming beach on Mahé: Beau Vallon Bay.
- Best surfing beach: Grand'Anse, Mahé.
- Best snorkelling beach: Port Launay (Marine Park).
- Best fly-fishing (saltwater bonefish): the lagoon, Alphonse atoll.
- Most photographed: Anse Source d'Argent, La Digue.
- Voted World's Best Beach: at least three in Seychelles.
- Best hideaway beaches: Petite Boileau Mahé and Anse La Blague, Praslin.
- Dangerous beaches May–October on Mahé: Grand'Anse, Anse Takamaka and Anse Intendance. And on La Digue: Grand and Petite Anse.

▲ *Above: The exquisite azure, turquoise and emerald green hues of Ste Anne Marine National Park.*
▶ *Opposite: Beau Vallon Bay, as pure as it gets.*

SILENT WORLD

Ghostly rays, angelfish, tiger cowries and a treasure trove of corals await the snorkeler merely by swimming offshore around the many islands of Seychelles. Go in two's, and the first tip is to spit in your mask to prevent misting. But you can also learn to dive with aqualungs at 22 dive centres, many rated PADI 5★. You'll start in a swimming pool before progressing to one of the 40 excellent sites around Mahé or even the gorgeous 'Desroches Drop' plateau in the Amirantes. The professional may play at depth with a spotted 15m (49ft) whale shark but the amateur could easily swim with a turtle off Bird Island.

Glacis is named after the giant weathered granite boulders that fall steeply to the sea along this stretch of coast. You can park at Manresa if you want to walk.

STE ANNE MARINE NATIONAL PARK ★★★

The largest of Mahé's offshore islands are the group facing Victoria within the boundary of Ste Anne Marine National Park. **Ste Anne's**, a mountain pyramid of an island right in front of Victoria harbour, was the site of the first French settlement in 1770. In those days the island was surrounded by mangroves, crocodiles roamed its forests, and dugongs swam off its quiet shores. It has been declared a private island to protect the marine park and, no doubt, to encourage exclusivity for the new 87-villa resort. Contact the Marine Parks Authority for landing permission and fees. A whaling station was set up there in 1832, and during World War II, a giant petroleum storage tank to service seaplanes. Visitors coming in to land at the airport have one of the best views of the park. The water is a kaleidoscope of blue, turquoise, opal and aquamarine amongst the coral reefs, submarine islands of seaweed and the open flats of white sand which fringe these pretty islands.

The waters of the park are shallow, safe, and rich in coral and sea life. The best underwater areas for fish and coral are off Anse Cimitière and Cabot on Ste Anne, and in a stretch running between **Moyenne** and

Round Island. The park and its islands are popular for day trips, with up to 35,000 people visiting it annually. One of the most interesting ways to see the spectacular underwater scenery is on a glass-keeled Mason's Travel boat in which you can sit and marvel at the wonders of the reef at your feet. There is a Conservation Information Centre on Round Island, and **restaurants** on Cerf, Round and Moyenne, where writer Brendon Grimshaw will trade pinch-of-sand tales of ghosts, buccaneer graves and buried treasure.

BEAU VALLON ★★★
A 'beautiful valley' couched between high mountains, Beau Vallon opens out onto a 6km (4-mile) bay stretching from Sunset Beach to the north all the way round to the granite cliffs of Bel Ombre, and incorporates an exquisite, mile-long scimitar beach. Shaded by huge *takamaka* trees, the talcum beach only 15 minutes over the mountain saddle from Victoria is the favourite with young muscled men in shades and tattoos. It has always been Seychelles' playground. There are a dozen hotels around the bay, and it is the heart of action fun: paragliding, water-skiing and diving are all on offer. For

GLIMPSES OF SEYCHELLES

Practically every vantage point in Seychelles is a 360° postcard.
● **Sans Souci pass:** a glimpse of paradise, the road out of Victoria towards Morne Seychellois National Park. A number of excellent viewpoints over the harbour, islands and town.
● **Le Niol:** if paragliding from the beach isn't your thing, this is the best view over Beau Vallon Bay.
● **Pirates Arms Hotel:** the best verandah in town for watching the laid-back life of Victoria go by.
● **Mission:** south Mahé's mountain forests, sea and sparkling coves. And further down, Thérèse and Conception islands.

TAMARIND AND ZAMALAKS

Year-round there are fruits to be picked in Seychelles. You will see fallen fruit everywhere: on the roads, the mountains, and in everyone's back yard. They include:

- Tamarind. Tangy, tasty fruit, like a brown brittle peashell. Makes a lovely drink.
- Karambol. Tart star-shaped fruit. The wood makes the best roundel for tambourine-shaped *moutya* drums
- Jackfruit. Grows on the trunk of trees. As big as a watermelon. Very rich and strong smelling.
- Red-skinned bananas. Big and fat. *Banan mil* are tiny breakfast treats. Huge *banan zak* are for cooking. There are 25 varieties of banana in Seychelles.
- Mango. The Indian king of fruits. Unripe it is made into a delicious salad with oil, vinegar, salt and pepper.
- Zamalak. White or red crispy fruits. Looks like a small apple. Good in jams and stewed.

those less energetic, all the poolside drinks are served in chilled sugar-rimmed glasses, and the sunsets behind Silhouette Island are stunning.

The days when the Northolme Hotel would proudly advertise 24-hour electricity and 'hot baths on request' have passed. Today's paradise *à la mode* has to include 'infinity' pools, tennis courts, boutiques, coffee shops, dancing and water sports. Yet, for all that, even the largest hotels are hidden among the trees and you will never see more than 200 people on the beach.

One Man on a Dead Man's Chest

Near the saddle of the pass on the road from Victoria to Beau Vallon, a road twisting off to the left leads up through the granite massif and dark breadfruit forest to Le Niol, which has sweeping, lonely views of the whole Beau Vallon Bay.

Down below, at the far western end of the crescent, is the beach and famous pirate treasure dig site at Bel Ombre. It seems terribly disappointing that a decent haul of treasure hasn't been found in Seychelles, as every palm-laced cove and azure beach seems to hint at hidden plunder, and there were certainly plenty of pirates, privateers and corsairs knocking around the islands down the years. Many of their descendants still live in Seychelles.

Grenadier Gaurdsmen **Reginald Cruise-Wilkins** came from England to settle at Beau Vallon in 1949, determined to find the treasure of cutthroat **Olivier le Vasseur**. *La Buze*, or the Buzzard, who ravaged the Indian Ocean in the 1770s, supposedly buried treasure worth £100 million at Bel Ombre before he felt the gallows noose tighten around his neck. He is said to have tossed a scrap of paper to the crowd on the scaffold calling, 'My treasure to he who will understand'. It was this cryptogram, based partially on the labours of Hercules, that Cruise-Wilkins believed he had mastered. Working with other documents supplied by locals, and encouraged by digs that had revealed strange rock markings and the corpses of two men with

◀ *Left: Mysterious, moody Le Niol mountain road, high above Bel Ombre (beautiful shadow) coast.*

earrings, he spent decades and considerable amounts of money digging, constructing sea dykes and removing rock. But with the exception of a few tantalizing clues – the trigger guard of a musket, a coin of Charles I's time, the stone statue of a woman, and a cavern with a trapdoor – he died disappointed. A pirate's flag used to fly over this corner of Bel Ombre by the side of the road where Cruise-Wilkins' son, John, has not yet abandoned hope.

Off the western end of Bel Ombre there is a walking path leading into the Morne Seychellois National Park, which traverses the cliff tops to a pretty little cove called **Anse Major**, the wildest area of North Mahé.

DON'T EAT THE CRABS

Marianne North, the indomitable Victorian artist and botanist whose superb paintings of flowers and plants hang in Victoria's Natural History Museum, landed on North Mahé in 1883. She dropped her bag and screamed with wonder at the fiddler crabs 'to the amazement of my porters who said coolly they were not good to eat'.

BEST TIMES TO VISIT

The cooler, drier months in Seychelles, are during the southeast trades from **April to September**. At all times of year, however, it is tropically warm and humid. It can rain at any time, but expect torrential downpours lasting several days over the **Christmas** period.

GETTING THERE

Air Seychelles flies from Johannesburg, six hubs (two in the Far East) and Mauritius. Air France, Air India, Air Mauritius, Kenya Airways, Emirates and Qatar also fly to Seychelles. British Airways has an office in Victoria but at the moment no flights. Port Victoria is the sole point of entry for yachts.
Transfers: Mason's Travel and other tour operators offer transfers, or there are taxis. If you don't have much luggage, there are inexpensive and regular buses. The airport is situated some 10km (6 miles) south of Victoria.

GETTING AROUND

Hire cars are by far the most popular way to explore the island. Remember, some of the roads are precipitous. There are some 40 rental companies in Seychelles. Try Hertz at the airport, or tel: 248 322447, e-mail: hertz@seychelles.net
Bicycles are best hired on rural Praslin and La Digue. **Bus:** Get a timetable and map from the Central Bus Terminal, tel: 248 224550 or 280280, corner 5th June Ave and Palm St. Platform and bus numbers don't necessarily correspond. Bus stop signs are written on the road. Daylight (and one night circular) service only. SR7 will take you anywhere. **Taxis:** Some have meters but there is an agreed fare structure. Check. Taxi Rank Victoria, tel: 248 322279. Operators' Association, tel: 248 323895.

WHERE TO STAY

Near Victoria
Apart from the Wharf there are no luxury hotels in Victoria.
Wharf Hotel/Marina, tel: 248 607700, e-mail: thewharf@seychelles.net website: www.wharfseychelles.com Luxury; 16 rooms.
Bel Air Hotel, tel: 248 224416, e-mail: belair@seychelles.net website: www.seychelles.net/belair Cool and colonial. Overlooking Victoria; 7 rooms.
Sunrise, tel: 248 224560, e-mail: sunrise@intelvision.net website: www.seychelles.net/sunrise-hotel Near Botanical Gardens; 16 rooms. Chinese cuisine and grocery shop.
La Sans Souci Guesthouse, tel: 248 225355, e-mail: sansouci@seychelles.net www.seychellessecrets.com Mountain road; three rooms, restaurant, babysitting.

Beau Vallon and Surrounds
Hilton Seychelles Northolme Resort and Spa, tel: 248 299179, e-mail: reservations.seychelles@hilton.com website: www.hiltonworldresorts.com 'Hot baths on request' the Northolme used to advertise 40 years ago. Today its 40 hill-perched rooms have jacuzzis, satellite TV and an 'infinity' pool.
Coral Strand, tel: 248 621000, e-mail: mail@coralstrand.sc website: www.coralstrand.com 140 rooms. Long-established family hotel situated on Beau Vallon beach.
Le Méridien Fisherman's Cove, tel: 248 677000, e-mail: salesfishcove@lemeridien.sc website: www.lemeridien.com/fishcove Magnificent Sokwe music; 70 rooms.

SMALL HOTELS
There are some 15 of these at Beau Vallon.
Daniella's Bungalows, Bel Ombre (west BVB), tel: 248 247914, e-mail: daniella@seychelles.net website: www.daniellasbungalows.com Near small stream; 12 rooms.

NORTH CIRCULAR
Manresa, N.E. Coast, tel: 248 241388, e-mail: manresa@email.sc Five air-conditioned rooms; Claudette and Nicholas have run it for 20 years; restaurant.
Bliss Hotel, Glacis, tel: 248 413169, e-mail: contact@bliss-hotel.net website: www.bliss-hotel.net Eight rooms.

ISLANDS
There are eight resorts on Ste Anne and especially Cerf

Island just offshore from Victoria, including the delightful **L'Habitation** (12 rooms), tel: 248 323111, e-mail: labicerf @seychelles.net website: www.seychelles.resa.com

WHERE TO EAT

Victoria

Pirates Arms, tel: 248 225001. Jam-packed, laid-back, people-watching eatery.
Marie Antoinette, St Louis Rd towards BVB, tel: 248 266222. Old Seychelles House. Has had the same Kreol menu (e.g. parrotfish fritters) for 33 years.
Rose Garden, Sans Souci Rd, tel: 248 225308. Thai cuisine, great views.

Beau Vallon

La Scala, Bel Ombre, tel: 248 247535. Superb mixed Kreol and Italian cuisine since 1978. Recommended.
Le Corsaire, Bel Ombre, tel: 248 247171. Seaside 'yo ho ho' and a grilled lobster. Great atmosphere.
La Perle Noire, Beau Vallon, tel: 248 620220. Italian; steaks.

There are many Kreolised restaurants, but the best Kreol food is at:
Boathouse, Beau Vallon, tel: 248 247898. Sand floor. Popular Kreol fish buffet.
Chez Gaby, Round Island Marine Park, tel: 248 322111. Lunches.
L'Habitation des Cerfs Luxury Hotel, Cerf Island, tel: 248 323111. Laid-back beachside eating.

TOURS AND EXCURSIONS

There are many combinations of tours and activities and many **tour operators** including the following:

Mason's Travel, Revolution Ave, tel: 248 288888, e-mail: info@masonstravel.com
Creole Travel Services, tel: 248 297000, e-mail: info@travelservices.com
7° South, Kingsgate House, tel: 248 292800, e-mail: 7south@seychelles.net

Excursions

Glass-bottomed reef boat, Ste Anne Marine Park. Contact Mason's Travel, tel: 248 288888.
Big Game Fishing. Contact Marine Charter, tel: 248 322126, e-mail: mca@seychelles.net
Island Cruising. *M.V. Indian Ocean Explorer*, seven cabins, tel: 248 225844, e-mail: info@ioexpl.com
Shamal, 50ft, three cabins, tel: 248 514735, e-mail: wworld@seychelles.net
Yacht Charter. Silhouette Cruises. Topsail schooners, tel: 248 324026, e-mail: cruises@seychelles.net
There are many others, particularly catamarans.
Helicopters Trips. Around Mahé and to 10 islands, tel: 248 385863, e-mail: info@helicopterseychelles.sc
Diving. There are many options. Try Dive Seychelles, Beau Vallon Bay Hotel, tel: 248 247165.

Fly-fishing. Particularly bonefish. Contact Marine Charter Association, near yacht club, tel: 248 322126.
Bird-watching. Contact Nature Seychelles, Roche Caiman, tel: 248 601100.
Package holidays. To avoid expense, your agent can package using high-density hotels like Berjaya Beau Vallon Bay.

USEFUL CONTACTS

Air Seychelles: tel: 248 384232.
Airport: tel: 248 381000.
Directory Enquiries: tel: 100.
Emergency: tel: 999.
Hospital: tel: 248 388000.
Doctor: try Dr Jivan, tel: 248 324008, or Dr Chetty, tel: 248 321911.
Dentist: tel: 248 224852.
Pharmacy: try Berhams, Victoria House Arcade, tel: 248 225559.
Optometrist: Micock Consulting, tel: 248 321177.
Tourist Information: tel: 248 610800, e-mail: info@seychelles.net website: www.seychelles.travel
Taxis: tel: 248 322279.
Car Rental: try Hertz (*see* Getting Around) or Tropicar, tel: 248 373336.
Conservation: try Nature Seychelles, tel: 248 601100, e-mail: nature@seychelles.net
Access to Islands: Cerf, La Digue, Mahé and Praslin are the main public islands, 14 others are private. They and others involve special permissions.

3
South and West Mahé

The southern and western areas of Mahé, caressed by the trade winds, are separated from Victoria and the main tourist areas by the island's central range of mountains. It was the last area to receive tarred roads, electricity and larger hotels, and with a myriad of hidden coves, coconut plantations and empty beaches, it is also the most rural and loveliest part of Mahé. Here you will find lone fishermen coming ashore to sell their catch of *karang* on the beach, deserted picnic coves, old plantation houses sleeping among the *zak* fruit and banana trees, people walking barefoot in the tiny villages, and old men on their way to the local store carrying palm-frond shopping bags. As always, the high, jungle-covered mountains brood above, offering cool, airy walks with wide views of hillside, reef and sparkling sea, while in the forests of Morne Seychellois National Park survives a living museum of unique and unusual plants and animals.

CENTRAL MAHÉ AND THE MOUNTAINS

The mountains of Mahé fall down to the sea in a riot of tropical greenery and dramatic black precipices. Rising abruptly out of the ocean, the mountains are almost constantly shrouded in swirling mist and flecked by bright sunlight, creating the dappled, eerie atmosphere of true montane forest, the hidden home of rare and exotic plants.

Morne Seychellois National Park covers about 30km² (12 sq miles), incorporating the highest of

CLIMATE

The climate of south and west Mahé is really no different from that of the north. The southeasterly **trade winds** buffet the south coast, adding to the lonely wildness of some of the coves. With mist swirling around, there is more chance of **rain** in the mountains and it's considerably cooler at night, hence La Misère being a choice residential area.

◀ *Opposite: Majestic granite mountains in Morne Seychellois National Park.*

DON'T MISS

*** Walks in the mountains, especially the exotic misty mountain walk known as Casse Dent (teeth-breaker) in the lea of Morne Seychellois, the highest mountain. The trail starts uphill from the tea factory.
*** Grand'Anse Beach: long, wild and beautiful.
** Snorkelling in Port Launay Marine Park.
** The chance to go exploring: 'grab-a-picnic-find-a-cove'.
** Anse Boileau and the marquetry ceiling in the church.
* Crafts Village Anse aux Pins: artists at work.

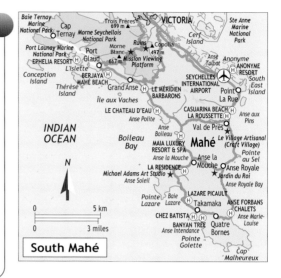

South Mahé

MOUNTAIN BIRD

The *payanke* (literally *paille en queue* – old straw tail), the white-tailed tropicbird, has two feathers that flow out 30cm (1ft) behind its large, white, streamlined body. They are sea birds whose preferred delicacies are squid or flying fish. Often seen in pairs, especially during the stiff-winged courtship flight (when the noise they make sounds almost like sneezing), they prefer to fish far out to sea. A quick and powerful flyer, the tropicbird seems to symbolize the space, freedom and beauty of all that is Seychelles.

Mahé's misty peaks and a large section of the western interior. The highest point is the mountain **Morne Seychellois** itself, at 905m (2970ft). There are no settlements and only one road through the park; it is all mountainous jungle, towering trees and mysterious nature. From Victoria, the **Sans Souci** mountain road over to Port Glaud cuts through the park, winding up the hillside and offering stunning views over the harbour and multi-pastel reef platforms below. It passes a number of interesting buildings, such as the American Embassy in a house called '1776', where Archbishop Makarios of Cyprus lived during his exile.

As the often precipitous road twists its way under the towering peaks, it passes the starting points for signposted walking trails which lead into the park and up to the peaks of **Trois Frères**, **Copolia** and **Morne Blanc** respectively.

At **Mission** there is a platform with spectacular views over the western coast, while on the descent into Port Glaud the **Tea Tavern** is a good place to sample and buy six different tea flavours including *citronelle* and cinnamon.

Morne Seychellois National Park

The park contains the best of the remaining indigenous forest of Seychelles, the giant lowland trees having been cut long ago, mainly to fuel cinnamon factories. There is something haunting and silently magnificent about the vast gothic cathedral of the forest. The canopy of trees soars 12m (39ft) above you as you walk, and all around green light plays on the **lichens**, **ferns**, straggling **creepers** and **old man's beard**. The best way to see the park beyond the road is to walk up one of the signposted paths. (Buy a trail map at Antigone in Victoria.) But it is advisable to go with an experienced guide. Be careful of deep cracks between boulders which are often hidden by the carpet of damp leaves, and sharp high drops often ending in swamps. There are nine trails in the national park.

Nearly all of the 70 or so endemic flowering plants and trees of Seychelles are found somewhere in the National Park: **screw pines**, **palms**, *koko maron* (the coconut tree named after a runaway slave), **orchids** and the **pitcher plant**. It is highly likely that Morne Seychellois is home to the total world population of both the ***bwa-d-fer*** (ironwood) and the jellyfish tree, ***bwa mediz***. This tree, which was sensationally rediscovered by botanists in 1970, is about 8m (26ft) high with tiny, rose-like flowers which become clusters of sunburnt fruit like upside-down parachutes, hence the name jellyfish.

MISSION

Just below the crest of the Forêt Noir (Black Forest) pass on the Sans Souci road there is a viewing platform overlooking tea and coffee plantations, called Mission. A hundred and fifty years ago it was a school, Venn's Town, for the children of the 2409 Africans rescued from Arab slavers by the 'gallantry of the British navy'. This was not unlike today's Somali pirates, two of whose ships were recently sunk by Seychelles naval gunboats. Restored and historically trail-mapped, an avenue of trees divides the deserted moss-covered ruins from the hush of the flanking forest. It is a gracious, quiet spot, with the sound of streams in the valley below, bees, and the pleasant scent of *citronelle* grass in the wind.

▼ *Below: Hideaway houses in the mountains.*

THE PITCHER PLANT

One of Seychelles' most famous plants, the pitcher plant has tendrils like a cup, or jug, with a lid, which contain an enzyme liquid. Insects are attracted by a sugary solution secreted by the plant, then slip down the smooth sides of the cup into the liquid, where they are trapped by the plant. Pitcher plants are found on Mahé and Silhouette, and are known to be of Asian, rather than African, origin: another small piece of evidence proving ancient continental links.

There are only about 11 trees still growing in the wild, so rare they merit their own genus.

Apart from the endemics, there are a lot of what botanists call exotics, not because they are spectacularly colourful, but because they are strangers. One example is the pale, grey-trunked *albizia* tree, which is common in Africa; another is the **cinnamon** bush, which has a sweet, pleasant smell if you crumple it in your hand.

Frogs such as the **pygmy piping frog**, which makes a lot of noise considering that it is only the size of a cowrie shell, are found in the wet uplands, and seven of Seychelles' unique birds make use of the high green canopy. You might spot the **Seychelles kestrel**, or the **bare-legged scops owl**, while the noisy **Seychelles bulbul** plays the same warning role as the African 'Go Away' bird.

Grand'Anse

Grand'Anse, on the west coast over the La Misère road, is a long curve of wave-lashed beach which is often completely deserted; in some ways it is even more attractive than Beau Vallon. Watched over by giant *takamaka* trees, its waters lie open to the wind and ocean without the barrier of reef common to many of Mahé's beaches. The dangerous ocean currents running off the beach claimed the life of Governor John Thorpe in 1961 as he was trying to rescue a child.

▶ Opposite: A clutch of yellowhusk drinking coconuts.
▼ Below: Grand'Anse beach is beautiful, but occasionally swept by dangerous currents.

During the southeast monsoon winds it is Seychelles' surfing beach.

There are less than 1000ha (2470 acres) of arable land in Seychelles. **The Ministry of Agriculture Research Station** farm at Grand'Anse specializes in researching a wide range of tropical fruits, with a view to increase their yield on the islands. Behind the strip of fertile land the mountains rise steeply into the Morne Seychellois National Park. This particular area is known as Grand Bois, which is believed to be a good place to find the elusive jellyfish tree, although you would need a guide to do so.

The aerials at the T-junction of the coastal road with the **La Misère** road belong to the BBC World Service Relay Station. Look out for the signs. Head northwest, and you will pass Grand'Anse and reach **Port Glaud** and the **Sans Souci** road. Beyond this on the coast are the marine national parks at **Port Launay** and **Baie Ternay**, where hawksbill turtles breed, and the green-backed heron, or *makak* in Kreol, is often spotted. Port Launay's expanse of palms and silent paths mark the abandoned and crumbling Seychelles National Youth Service Camp, scheduled to be an exclusive Emirates Airlines resort at some stage.

Standing off the coast at this point are the two substantial islands of **Thérèse** and **Conception**. The latter has no beach but Thérèse is popular with picnickers from the Mahé Beach Hotel, which has no beach and had to make one from scratch. In front of Thérèse, the tiny **L'Islette** is a delightful spot sitting in the middle of the cove where the Mare aux Cochons river emerges. The *Zwazo Banann* or *Linet* (White Eye) is a LBJ (Little Brown Job) and critically endangered. The world's last remaining 300 are found on Conception, with 31 successfully transferred to Frégate.

WEDDING IN PARADISE

Islands of love, Garden of Eden, frangipanis and whispering palms. It all started in the 1970s on fabulous Bird Island. Couples booked an all-inclusive civil wedding package and were married barefoot in the surf at sunset. Now many tour operators and large hotels offer the same. Book four months in advance, and bring all legal certificates. Church weddings can also be arranged but involve a bit more groundwork, and have to be in addition to the civil ceremony. You have to live in Seychelles for a minimum of three days before the wedding. Unlike Las Vegas – but then marriage is more of a gamble there.

SOUTH AND WEST MAHÉ

Barbarons

Barbarons is a low-lying plateau south of Grand'Anse which rises gradually from the coast through lush coconut plantations to a height of 600m (1970ft). Reef and rock lie close inshore with a wild and beautiful beach, somewhat obscured by a multi-room yellow-roofed resort, **Le Méridien Barbarons**. A little further is the **Chateau d'Eau**, a delightfully elegant French plantation house and small hotel.

An **orchid nursery** run by the Seychelles Marketing Board is nearby. Orchids grow well in Seychelles and there are some 25 local varieties, many of which are endemic. The farm is unfortunately not open to visitors.

ORCHIDS

Worldwide there are 17,000 species of orchid. Seychelles is home to 25, most of them epiphitic, meaning that they grow on other plants.
- Wild *payanke* or tropicbird orchid, the national flower.
- Wild vanilla orchid: large white flowers with an orange peach centre that bloom after rain and die by noon. There is no vanilla in them.
- Orchid tree: pink and mauve flowers. The seeds of some varietals are occasionally used for coffee.
- Phaius, or ground forest orchid, with leaves over 30cm (1ft) in length.
- Cultivated vanilla: pale green flowers and thick leaves on vines zigzagging up stakes. Big business in Seychelles 100 years ago, deforested slopes are witness to its popularity. Today it largely grows wild on trees.

THE SOUTH

Hidden coves with steep, twisty roads leading to them are a feature of South Mahé, and there always seems to be a charming little village behind these hidden gems. Some of the beaches are less than 50m (55yd) long and usually backed by heavy stands of *takamaka* trees leaning over the waters. It is in the south that the last *moutyas* were danced, *kasye* fishing traps lean up against trees, spoken English is more unusual, and domino players will gather in noisy groups in the villages. To this day folk from Anse Soleil or Quatre Bornes are regarded by the sophisticates of Victoria as coming from the sticks.

Anse Boileau

For many years it was thought that Lazare Picault, the first Frenchman to land in Seychelles, had done so in the bay named after him in South Mahé, where the Plantation Club is now owned by a Middle Eastern sheikh. (So they say.) In fact, Picault came ashore in the much more practical – for anchoring both sailing ship and beach-bound longboat – Boileau Bay, slightly further north. An ancient anchor above the beach serves as a memorial of his arrival.

A drive along the length of the bay leads past spindly coconut trees to the handsome, 160-year-old church of **Notre Dame de Sept Douleurs** (Our Lady of Seven Sorrows), which has some magnificent hardwood marquetry covering both the high ceiling and its support columns in mottled, chevron zigzag patterns. The altar crucifixion tableau is as gory as any pious 19th-century self-flagellating artist could devise.

From the shallow tidal waters of Anse Boileau beach, the coastal mountains stretch left and right like enveloping bird wings, in a lush panorama that prompted Picault to name Mahé the 'Isle of Abundance'. Part of the forest by the **Montagne Posée** mountain road is still known as L'Abondance. There is a trail which starts by the Cable and Wireless Station near **Bon Espoir** at the top of the pass and leads to a summit of 501m (1644ft). Anse Boileau's hinterland is

MOUNTAIN ROADS

There are six main passes over the mountains and many unmarked narrow ones. Just turn up any concrete road and explore. The smaller the mountain road, the more old, rural Seychelles.

- **Sans Souci:** from Victoria through Morne Seychellois National Park.
- **La Misère:** Plaisance to Grand'Anse.
- **Montagne Posée:** from Anse aux Pins
- **Les Canelles:** from Anse Royale to Anse La Mouche. Stop at Le Jardin du Roi.
- **Quatre Bornes:** Banyan Tree road. Fruit and roadside barbecues.
- **Adventure tip:** turn right at the yellow shop 1.6km (1 mile) south of Anse Royale Church through Val d'Endor. Comes out at Harvey's store.

◄◄ *Opposite: Thérèse and Conception Islands seen from above Port Glaud.*
◄ *Left: Intricate multi-wood marquetry decorates the secret interior of the lovely Church of the Seven Sorrows at Anse Boileau.*

▲ *Above: Facing Souris or Mouse Island, a favourite cove for families.*

FORESTS OF THE SEA

Care to do the Mangrove Board Walk? No, it's not a dance but a man-made deck in the mangrove wildlife wetlands near Gand'Anse, Mahé. From the view platform you can spy crabs, fish and breeding birds. The stilt-like roots of mangroves march forth in the mud throwing out shoots, reclaiming land. Mangrove, *mangliye* in Kreol, comes from a Bahamas-Indian word. Aldabra has 800ha (1979 acres) of mangroves, co-nesting perches for squadrons of red-footed boobies and their usual enemies, frigate birds. There are *inter alia* red, white and black mangroves. Denude shorelines of their grip to build yacht marinas, and tsunamis become more destructive.

agricultural with an orchid nursery, and further south the Barbaron Botanical Gardens is due to open in 2010. At Anse La Mouche, stop for a meal at **La Sirene** or **Anchor Café**. Ask for fish or any Seychelles fish curry. They are all tasty.

Corsair Country

In the hook of **Anse la Mouche**, there is a magnificent panorama of the whole of west Mahé – a great long tumble of mountain, cloud and sea. Other than the lofty perch of Mission in the hills there is probably no grander view on Mahé. Perhaps it is the reason why the Hodoul family settled in this area generations ago.

Mention the name of sea captain **Jean François Hodoul** to an old Seychellois and you'll probably notice a faint shiver. An adventurer and successful privateer, 'Le Corsair' was also a man of refined and sophisticated tastes, reputed to have the best table in Seychelles. A tiny island in Victoria's yacht basin and a smidgen of Aldabra atoll are named Hodoul. A local almanac of 1819 records that Hodoul '… ravaged the Red Sea, Gulf of Persia, Malabar and Coromandel Coasts, Sumatra and Java', yet Seychelles was always his base. He settled down to run his estates initially in Silhouette, then Beau Vallon, before moving to

Mamelles, just south of Victoria, where his great mansion still stands.

His descendants feature regularly in the history of the islands and in politics. The family house at Anse la Mouche is near 'La Residence' holiday villas, built by Marie-Anne Hodoul, the great-granddaughter of the corsair.

This area of the south coast used to have several old plantation houses. These venerable gems are fast decaying or disappearing in Seychelles – a great loss. Coral raised verandahs, rusty tin roofs and big wooden exteriors are hidden from the beach among flowers and thick greenery. If you are not a beach person, wander from cove to cove, spot one of the old beauties, abandoned, shutters closed and ravaged by salt winds. One of the charms of these houses, particularly on La Digue, was that almost every one was a living museum with a treasure trove of historical artefacts. British civil servants were fond of denigrating the planters, but in an agriculturally hostile environment it was always a struggle to introduce and sustain new crops, plants and animals. They did, however, have pawpaws, coconuts, breadfruit, spices, tamarinds and their stern God to sustain them. And the sort of views you get at Anse la Mouche.

PLANTATION HOUSES

Some of the unusual features that you can still find in Seychelles plantation houses:
- Sweeping steps up to the verandah made of coral.
- Flower displays atop a polished trunk of coco de mer.
- Wide rattan lounge chairs with crocheted antimacassars.
- *Garde manger:* a wire-meshed box hanging in the kitchen from the roof to deter rats, with a cone of water suspended around the cord to combat ants.
- *Grenier:* granary in the loft. Separate window entrance to winch up maize, rice or coffee.
- *Gargoulet:* water jug.
- *Boulwar:* iron kettle.

▼ *Below: A hidden mountain cottage, but with today's vital accessory, a TV antenna.*

The Southern Tip

As the road turns out of Anse la Mouche over to **Baie Lazare**, you will find the studio of famous Seychelles artist Michael Adams overlooking **Anse aux Poules Bleues**. A little further on there is a broken road which leads to **Anse Soleil**'s tiny, sunset-shimmering beach. There used to be an old sugar cane mill in the forest. Now there is a small hotel and tiny café.

After Takamaka, just off the road before Quatre Bornes village, there is a handsome 110-year-old plantation house, the only thatched double-storey one still standing in Seychelles, the rest having adopted corrugated iron decades ago.

At the top of the saddle the road comes to **Quatre Bornes,** or four milestone village, with its brightly coloured shops hanging over the road. (Try the *moutay*, a *koeksister*-like honey snack.) Visit any of these little southern villages on a Sunday and you'll see the scenes of old-fashioned, rural Mahé: football games in the dusty road, quartets of hand-slapping domino players beneath the mango trees, neighbours sitting and chatting by their front porch, and washing laid out on the grass to dry.

From Quatre Bornes a narrow, twisting road leads to what used to be called Southern Seas, a 101ha (250-acre)

◄ *Left: Mangrove wetland rich in small wildlife, near Grand'Anse.*
◄◄ *Opposite: The only thatched double-storey plantation house still standing, after 100 years, in Seychelles.*

wild and windswept wilderness garden at Petite Boileau. This is Seychelles, its birds, trees and countryside as it was 50 years ago. Perfect solitude. For some reason it is closed – a billionaire developer no doubt has a beady spyglass on it. The small lonely bays, with no reefs to negotiate, are not protected from the shifting currents that sweep around this wild coast, land's end of Mahé.

Jardin du Roi

Some 200 years ago, **Pierre Poivre**, administrator of the Isle de France (the name at the time for Mauritius), sponsored an expedition to Seychelles to set up a spice nursery. He believed that conditions in Mahé might allow the crops to compete with those fabulous spices of the east that the Dutch had monopolized for so long.

The spot chosen for the garden was on a broad, low-lying plain of rich black soil well watered by two rivers, just up from the longest beach on the island called **Anse Royale**, in the southeast of Mahé. The nursery developed gradually, first rivalling the earlier, private venture at the settlement on Ste Anne's Island, and eventually replacing it. Within eight years they had cultivated cloves, nutmeg and pepper brought in from the Moluccas in Indonesia, and cinnamon from Ceylon.

WALKS

Information on walks and trails is available from e.g. Mason's Travel and from Antigone bookshop in Victoria; also complimentary maps. There are nine walks, all marked with pictograms.
- **No 2. Glacis Trois Frères**. In Morne Seychellois National Park, a trail to the top of Trois Frères (699m; 2293ft), the second-highest massif on the island. Start near Sans Souci Forestry Station. Spectacular views, but beware of cloud and do not stray from path. 4–5 hours.
- **No 8. Casse Dent**. Near Mission through Forêt Noire passing Morne Seychellois.
- **No 6. Morne Blanc** (667m; 2188ft). Start a little further down, nearer the Tea Factory. Morne Blanc cliff drops 250m (820ft). 4–5 hours.
- **No 7. Copolia**. Eastern side of Sans Souci road, past the forest station. Up to a height of 497m (1631ft). 3 hours.
- **Summit of Mt Brulée** between Anse Boileau and Anse aux Pins.
- **Bel Ombre** coast to Anse Major.

▲ *Above: Jardin du Roi's plantation house museum (and cinnamon ices), a favourite with school kids.*

CINNAMON

Cinnamon (an old Hebrew word) grows wild all over Seychelles. The spice was introduced at the Jardin du Roi on Mahé in 1772 and, of all the spice trees, has proved to be the most successful. Economically insignificant today, 40 years ago it provided 30% of Seychelles' foreign currency. Use it on pancakes, in jams, stews, or pluck a leaf and suck it as a pick-me-up. Buy bark rolls or quills in the market. In days past a brown-stained stream flowing down a beach meant distillation.

The nursery was deliberately burnt to the ground in 1780 when the farmers were told a British ship was sailing into Port Royale (Victoria) harbour, as the secrets of the spices were too valuable to fall into the enemy's hands. The man o' war turned out to be French.

In 1994, three young Seychellois with a sense of history opened their own Jardin du Roi at Anse Royale. Run by Micheline Georges, whose family has farmed this area since 1854 (with a special stamp for each vanilla pod), the gardens of 32ha (79 acres) are planted not only with the original spices but such modern additions as cardamom and the 19th-century money-spinner patchouli. It is a great spot to wander among the scented trees and flowers. Sunday lunch in the creperie is tops, especially the home-made spices ice cream. You'll see the old plantation house, museum, spices shop and reptile house. From the hill above the garden, Roche Gratte Fesse (literally 'scratch your bum rock'), there are splendid views of Anse Royale's beach, village and the towers of the two churches built right on the beach, one Anglican (built in 1889 by Englishman Mr Green – first owner of the Jardin du Roi property) and the other Catholic (built in 1854 and refurbished in 1931).

Anse aux Pins

Just around the corner from the airport, Anse aux Pins is a busy, crowded village and the home of the Reef, Seychelles' first big tourist hotel, now almost abandoned. Close-in reef stretches past the village to the casuarina-tufted **Pointe au Sel**, 6km (3.5 miles) distant. The rumble of the breakers can be heard night and day, as the thin, pine-like *filão* that give the beach its name fret in the trades – although the trees aren't in fact true pines at all.

Being close to the airport, this bay is often the last view visitors have of Seychelles, as their jet gains altitude above the emerald sea. Fifty years ago, there were only eight – all rustic – hotels in Seychelles. Now there are 140. Three of the original ones, Pirates Arms, Sunset and Northolme, are still functioning. Anse Aux Pins, being near the airport, saw the first tourist-boom hotels. Eleven still flourish there. There is a nine-hole golf course here, the only one on Mahé.

La Marine, where replicas of old French sailing boats are carved, the Craft Village, and Vye Marmit restaurant and old plantation house museum shouldn't be missed. The **Kreol Instititi** for furthering the language and culture of Seychelles is housed in an old plantation house called Maison St Joseph halfway down the bay. The beach is not the best as the reef is too close – although it can be good for finding octopus.

ON THE MOVE

There are some 500km (311 miles) of surfaced roads in Seychelles, and some 11,000 motor vehicles of which 300 are taxis, 1100 self-drive and 200 buses, the main form of transport. The days of rickshas, *pousse*, have long passed, as have the flat-bottomed pirogue canoes that waited 'for madam' like carriages in the shallows at dinner parties. Now the waters are graced by catamarans, the occasional helicopter shuttle above and Toyotas on the new double highway to the airport.

▼ *Below: Spiritual solitude in the lea of Anse Royale's twice renovated church.*

For further information see also North Mahé at a Glance (pp54–55)

BEST TIMES TO VISIT

It rains heavily in **December**, **January** and **February**, while the southeast trade winds from **April** to **October** bring refreshing breezes to all but the northwest of the island. The temperature stays at a steady 27°C (81°F) all year, with a tropical humidity of 80–85%. Many hotels have air conditioning; others, cool fans and large shuttered windows.

GETTING THERE

Other than cruise ships or your own yacht, the only way to get to Mahé is to **fly**. There are scheduled services from Africa (Johannesburg and Nairobi), Europe, and the Middle and Far East. The international airport is on the east coast of Mahé, a 15-minute drive from Victoria. Airport **transfers** are usually organized by Mason's or tour operators.

GETTING AROUND

Car hire is the favourite for touring the rural areas of Mahé. There are practically no gravel roads left, and plenty of passes over the mountains. These are steep, winding roads with marvellous views of forest and shore far below. Beware of steep drops off the narrow roads, and tight corners. The speed limit is 65kph (40kph in towns and villages). There are not many petrol stations. Make sure you fill up or you'll pay a premium. And hire cars come with an empty tank.

Taxis are available in Victoria, the airport, and at the larger hotels; 24-hour service. Note that taxi fares are relatively expensive. One of the best ways to get around is on the local **buses**. The service is cheap and regular but they don't operate after 19:00. A **regular bus service** is available around the beaches and villages of South Mahé and over the mountains. Call out 'devan' ('up ahead') when you want to disembark.

WHERE TO STAY

The large, often high-density holiday hotels are sited on the best beaches. They include:
Four Seasons Resort Petite Anse, tel: 248 393321, e-mail: res.seychelles@fourseasons.com website: www.fourseasons.com/seychelles/preview 80 villas. Stunning luxury.
Maia Luxury Resort, Anse Louis, tel: 248 390000, e-mail: reservations@southernsun.sc website: www.maia.com.sc Spa, 30 rooms, 300 species of garden plants. Perfection.
Banyan Tree, Intendance, tel: 248 385500, e-mail: reservations-seychelles@banyantree.com website: www.banyantree.com 47 villas, costing up to US$4500 per villa – 'fraid so! Each villa, however, has its own pool, jacuzzi and steam room.

SMALL AND BUDGET HOTELS
Note: The smaller the hotel, the better it tends to be.

Lazare Picault, Anse Gaulettes, tel: 248 361111, e-mail: lazarpco@seychelles.net web: www.lazarepicaulthotel.com Gorgeous sea views, 14 chalets.
Le Relax, Anse Royale, tel: 248 382900, e-mail: helpdesk@lerelaxhotel.com www.lerelaxhotel.com Lovely boutique hotel, 10 rooms.
La Residence, Anse La Mouche, tel: 248 371733, e-mail: villa@seychelles.net Three villas, five studios.
Xanadu, Southern tip, tel: 248 366522, e-mail: xanadu@seychelles.net Eight villas.
Chalets d'Anse Forbans, tel: 248 366111, e-mail: info@forbans.com website: www.forbans.com 14 self-catering beach chalets. Recommended.
Le Chateau d'Eau, Barbarons, tel: 248 378177, fax: 248 378388. Five rooms, plantation elegance.
Hotel La Roussette, Anse aux Pins, tel: 248 376245, e-mail: manager@hotel-larousette.com www.Hotel-LaRoussette.com 5 bungalows. Recommended.
Pied Dans L'eau, Anse Royale, tel: 248 430110, e-mail: piedanslo@intelvision.net web: www.piedansleau.sc Six de luxe self-catering apartments.

WHERE TO EAT

Carefree, Anse aux Pins, tel: 248 375237. First small hotel in Seychelles (built in 1971). Run by Zita and Leon Monthy. Kreol cuisine.
Casuarina, right on Anse aux Pins beach, tel: 248 376211.

For further information see also North Mahé at a Glance (pp54–55)

Open 'macouti' thatch.

Chez Batista's, Takamaka Beach, tel: 248 366300. Sand in her feet, frangipani in her hair. Seats 200.

Vye Marmit, Pomme Cannelle, Au Cap, East Coast, tel: 248 376155. In Val des Près craft village. Set menu, almost forgotten Kreol dishes. Recommended.

Kaz Kreol Pizzeria, Anse Royale Beach, tel: 248 371680. Closed Mondays.

Le Reduit, Takamaka, tel: 248 366116. Laid-back beach curries, great views.

La Sirene, Anse Poules Bleues, tel: 248 361339. Lunches only. Near Michael Adams' art studio overlooking Anse La Mouche.

Chez Plume, Anse Boileau, tel: 248 355050. Tasty Kreol specialities served here.

Les Dauphins Heureux, Anse Royale, tel: 248 430100. Elegant seashore dining.

What to Eat

A good bet is octopus curry, and also fruit bat paté, raw mango salad, palmis, breadfruit in coconut milk, grilled kordonnyen, or tectec soup. Try the bananas in syrup.

TOURS AND EXCURSIONS

Bird-watching. Contact Nature Seychelles, Birdlife International, tel: 248 601100. Buy Adrian Skerrett's books. Incidentally, the noisy whistler is the Indian mynah.

Golf. Reef, Anse aux Pins, tel: 248 376234.

Walking Trails. Contact the Tourist Office in Independence House, Victoria for trail maps of Morne Seychellois National Park, or Antigone Bookshop, Victoria House Arcade, tel: 248 225443, or any tour operator.

Diving. Any local large hotel, or Island Ventures Dive Seychelles PADI 5★, Beau Vallon Bay Hotel, tel: 248 345445. There are 10 good dive sites off West Mahé including Baie Ternay Marine Park.

Dancing. The larger hotels feature sega music and dancing displays, usually at weekends.

Tennis. Large hotels.

Fishing. Contact Marine Charter, tel: 248 322126. Small beach fishermen may take you out in their boat.

Helicopter Scenic Trips. For a great view of paradise, tel: 248 385863. There are 10 helipads in Seychelles.

Reef Exploring. Wear a pair of tough shoes and wade or swim to the reef at low tide, or go by boat. Don't snorkel alone, never collect live shells or coral, and be wary of spiky black sea urchins.

Swimming. Seychellois tend to overplay swimming dangers. But be wary at Intendance, Anse Takamaka and Grand'Anse. During May–October there are strong currents, waves and winds.

USEFUL CONTACTS

Air Seychelles: tel: 248 384232.
Airport: tel: 248 381000
Directory Enquiries: tel: 100.
Emergency: tel: 999.
Doctor: try Dr Jivan, tel: 248 324008, or Dr Chetty, tel: 248 321911.
Dentist: tel: 248 224852.
Pharmacy: try Berhams, Victoria House Arcade, tel: 248 225559.
Optometrist: Micock Consulting, tel: 248 321177.
Tourist Information: tel: 248 610800, e-mail: info@seychelles.net, website: www.seychelles.travel
Taxis: tel: 248 322279.
Car Rental: try Palm Cars, tel: 248 712102, or Hertz, tel: 248 322447, web: www.seychelles.net/hertz
Access to Islands: Cerf, La Digue, Mahé and Praslin are the main public islands, 14 others are private. They and others involve special permissions.

GRAND'ANSE	J	F	M	A	M	J	J	A	S	O	N	D
AVERAGE TEMP. °F	81	82	82	82	82	81	79	79	79	81	81	79
AVERAGE TEMP. °C	27	27.5	28	28	28	27	26	26	26.5	27	27	26.5
SEA TEMP. °F	82	80	82	80	78	77	73	73	73	79	77	80
SEA TEMP. °C	28	27	28	27	26	25	23	23	23	26	25	27
RAINFALL in	17	7	25	7	9	6	5	7	7	9	9	11
RAINFALL mm	422	180	237	175	233	146	130	170	169	225	233	274
Days of Rainfall	11	6	7	6	8	6	6	6	7	6	8	10

4
Praslin

For many people, the island of Praslin is the real Seychelles. A rural, languid island of beaches, palms, and country roads, it has all the ingredients of the Garden of Eden image that made Seychelles famous. High in the hills, the **Vallée de Mai** is home to the 100ft tall coco de mer palms that bear the largest fruit in the world. Theories have suggested that the giant palms are the biblical trees of Adam and Eve, and the valley the paradise that man was heir to before being tempted into mortality.

Sited 40km (25 miles) east of Mahé, Praslin is the archipelago's second largest island, 11km (7 miles) long and 4km (2.5 miles) wide. It is the choice holiday spot of Seychellois themselves, and visitors who have discovered it tend not to linger too long at Mahé airport as they transfer to one of the small Otter aircraft that make the 15-minute hop across the ocean.

Praslin's highest peak, at 367m (1204ft), is only a third that of Morne Seychellois on Mahé, and its population is just over 7000 people. There are no towns, and only two villages, at **Grand'Anse** and **Baie Ste Anne** where the old-fashioned schooners tie up. But even in these quaint settlements you never get the impression of there being many people around, for Praslin is laid-back, relaxed and unspoilt in every way. The pace of life encourages you to explore on foot, to a distant beach, up the trails in the hills, or simply along to a lone corner shop on the Anse Kerlan road. You may well meet one of the eccentric and interesting

◀ *Opposite: Cool crystal waters, Praslin.*

73

PRASLIN

DON'T MISS

*** Vallée de Mai, home of the coco de mer fruit and palms. World Heritage Site. Trails and curio shop.

*** A visit to Café des Arts art gallery. Paintings and crafts by Seychelles artists.

*** Côte d'Or beach. Refuge for fruit bats. Traditional Craft Museum.

** Bicycle ride around the mainly flat circular road from Côte d'Or to Baie Ste Anne, Consolation, Grand'Anse and Anse Kerlan.

** Dive or snorkel in the Marine Park in Curieuse Bay.

* Explore Grand'Anse Village and **Baie Ste Anne**.

* Walk to Anse Volbert or **Baie Chevalier**.

artists, writers and bohemians the island seems to attract, and come to understand the depth of affection in an old island song. 'Praslin, *mon* Praslin,' it goes, 'I will never let you go'.

The economy of Praslin was founded for many years on coconut, vanilla and patchouli plantations, fishing, and quarrying (Praslin's red granite is prized for building façades on Mahé), but increasingly the island has set its foundations in tourism. Originally keen to maintain the number of hotels on Praslin at an ecologically sustainable level, the government has unfortunately been seduced by the siren lure of 'development'.

AROUND PRASLIN

Grand'Anse

Grand'Anse is and always has been the bohemian backwater of Seychelles. It is on the western side of Praslin, but remains exposed to the trade winds that come thrashing through the palms, with waves tearing endlessly at the long line of reef far out to sea. The first hotel on Praslin, known as Grand'Anse Ideal Home, was followed by a thatched two-roomed bungalow

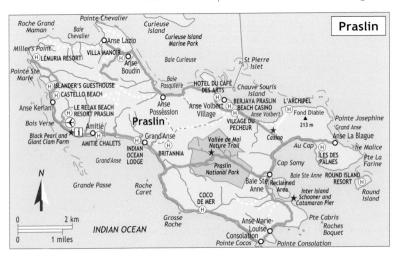

◀ *Left: Solitary fishing boat captured in the sunset at Grand'Anse.*

used by the visiting Mahé doctor on his rounds of the islands. The latter is still there after 40 years, though now refurbished and part of a lovely series of luxury duplex chalets on the beach called Indian Ocean Lodge. In the early days it was given the glamorous name of Mickey Mouse – and one of the guests over the years was another Hollywood star, Ronald Reagan.

With a dozen establishments such as Beach Villa, the venerable Britannia and the Jungle Nightclub ('as wild as it gets'), the village seems almost deliberately to cultivate a rakish bottle-of-rum ambience. Apart from the smart Barclays Bank and a new arcade, many of the colourfully painted tin-roofed buildings look as if they might fall over at any moment. There's a fish market, a plantation house, a tiny library, post office, and Janessa's polka-dot boutique. Peaking over the palms is the steeple of **St Matthew the Apostle**, a church dedicated in 1859, while the coco de mer-crested independence monument is a favourite place to stop, chat and have a beer.

Grand'Anse is not a good swimming beach by Seychelles' superlative standards (beware sandflies), but the long seaweed-strewn stretch of sand is a favourite with beachcombers. Between the sea and the hills a wide plain with coconut trees wafts back from the narrow road that hides the occasional house and the handsome bell tower of **St Joseph's** (1854) church.

▲ *Above: Yachts and pleasure craft at Baie Ste Anne's schooner jetty. The jetty is soon to be enlarged to accommodate cruise ships.*
▶ *Opposite: Anse La Blague (Cove of Tricks), south Praslin.*

Baie Ste Anne

Just behind Grand'Anse stands the central ridge of Praslin's hills with their distinctive patches of red granite soil. The mountains were once covered in huge forests but sadly fire ravaged them long ago. The main road of the island climbs through the hills, passing the entrance to the Vallée de Mai near the summit, before descending towards the sweeping curve of Baie Ste Anne.

Baie Ste Anne is the capital of Praslin, if such an expression can be justified by this sleepy seaside village, with its little cluster of small shops, school, hospital and power plant. On the beachfront you might still see men climbing the coconut trees to extract *calou* toddy. The spider-scramble up the trees that young men used to perform is rare these days, so look out for the trees with ladders leaning against them.

The village has always been a wooden boat-building centre and is the landing stage for the inter-island schooners from Mahé and La Digue and the fast 150-seater Cat Cocos ferry. The schooner to Mahé takes about three hours and is great fun especially when the crew troll for their lunch. There are usually two sailings daily. Baie Ste Anne, like Mahé's eastern flank, has had to suffer the indignity of reclamation off its sea wall but arriving at Baie Ste Anne from the sea is always a lovely sight, with the wide sweep of the sparkling bay, the fishing boats anchored, and the green rise up to the mysterious forest behind.

Go Local

Where is this bus going?	*Kote sa bis pe ale?*
Are you going to the Vallée de Mai?	*Ou pe al Vale d'Me?*
Is this our boat for La Digue?	*Sa nou bato pour La Digue?*
Is Anse Kerlan far?	*I lwen Anse Kerlan?*
Can you play moutya?	*Ou konn zwe moutya?*
What is this beach called?	*Kimanyer sa lans i apele?*
What is this fish called?	*Kimanyer sa pwason i apele?*

Côte d'Or

Côte d'Or along the shores of Anse Volbert bay is a 4km (2½-mile) expanse of soft white sand fringed with palms and yellow sea hibiscus. These flowers have a deep purple centre which turns orange by afternoon. Côte d'Or has a string of hotels, the **Casino des Îles** (Salon Privé, chemmy, slots) and umpteen small hotels and holiday activities along 'the strip' including wind-surfing, sailing, diving and snorkelling trips to nearby **Curieuse Island Marine Park**. You can even explore the depths on a night dive if you would like to see spiny red lobsters – who normally hide beneath their rock overhangs – strolling along. Tiny Chauvre Souris (Fruit Bat Island), one of two so named in Seychelles, stands a few metres off the beach.

Hidden from the larger hotels is the **Café des Arts**, and along the main road near Acajou Hotel is the lovely Traditional Craft Museum. Praslin is a perfect place for painters – full of empty country roads, relaxed villages, red hills, distant islands and a deserted beach at the end of each winding track. A number of artists live on

FRUIT BAT

The endemic flying fox or *chauve souris* looks like something out of Dracula, though close up it resembles a little brown furry fox.

● Unlike other bats, the *chauve souris* (literally, it means skittermouse) sees very well.

● Unlike other bats, it eats no insects or meat at all, only fruit.

● It has a wingspread of 1m (3.5ft).

● They cannot echo locate like other bats.

● Fruit bats play a major role in the reproduction of plants in Seychelles by disseminating fruit seed.

● Fruit bat is eaten as a delicacy in Seychelles. Beware Dracula's revenge.

PRASLIN

▲ *Above: North Praslin's 'Zimbabwe' wilderness.*

Praslin, and many more make it their holiday retreat. The Café des Arts used to be run by artist Christine Harter, whose gallery actively encourages all the visual arts in the islands. The café is also a popular meeting place, with its Parisian ambience and views out over the azure waters of the never-ending ocean.

Situated towards the eastern end of Côte d'Or is a large agricultural estate with palms, casuarina trees, mahoganies and browsing cattle. Set on stone pillars in one corner of the estate is the tiny house that once belonged to Henri Dauban (*see* panel, page 109) who did so much experimenting with and development of farming techniques on this long, tree-filled flatland. A mangrove swamp survives in the corner, with crabs digging around in the cracked mud and small red, white and blue flowers growing on the sandy pathways. The birds fluttering at your feet are the *toutrel coco* or barred ground dove, supposed to bring peace and good luck.

A long, isolated road goes past stands of passion fruit with their green, egg-shaped fruit and white tendril flowers, and reaches the elegant Archipel villas. From here a path leads along the wild and rocky coast around **Devil's Peak**, or Fond Diable ('fond', is an old French word meaning crown). This leads to delightful Anse La Blague which faces, across the reef, a coterie of lovely islands: Félicité, Petite Soeur, Grande Soeur, Île Cocos and the larger island of La Digue. A gear-challenging forested road leads over the hills from here to Baie Ste Anne.

CONSERVATIONISTS

For centuries, nature was considered boundless by the inhabitants of Seychelles. In 1769 Abbé Alexis Rochon was the first scientist to visit the islands, and in 1788 the first true conservationist arrived, the administrator Jean Baptiste Philogene de Malavois. He made recommendations for the protection of Seychelles' timber, tortoises and turtles. None heeded. Victorian artist Marianne North, Botanical Gardens director Paul Dupont, researcher Dr John Bradley in the 1930s and Seychellois such as Guy Lionnet, Jivan Shah, Justin Gerlach, Cousine Island conservationists, and Adrian and Judith Skerrett have much encouraged interest in Seychelles' flora and fauna. As have historians AWT Webb and William McAteer.

VALLÉE DE MAI

Though Praslin is generously blessed with stunning beaches and a wonderfully laid-back atmosphere, the peculiar attraction of the island is to be found in a small area of thick forest high up in the green hills. Here the famous **coco de mer** tree has its last natural habitat, in a valley of 4000 slumbering giants known as the Vallée de Mai (though often abbreviated to Val de Mai). The Vallée, an area of only 18ha (45 acres) enclosed within Praslin National Park's larger 338ha (835 acres), is a World Heritage Site, one of only two in Seychelles.

The whole national park area was so remote and mountainous that it remained totally untouched until the 1930s – a saving grace for the indigenous trees. Trail leaflets lead you to some of these, including the *bwa rouz*, with leaves like corrugated cardboard, and *northea kapisen*, with its horizontal cracked-mud bark. The new Information Centre at the entrance to the reserve is where the well-laid-out circular path begins. The car park and Information Centre are approximately halfway along the mountain road between Grand'Anse and Baie Ste Anne.

Fifty-two of Seychelles' indigenous plants and trees can be seen in this extraordinary valley, including all six endemic palm species. It is the last habitat of the unique **black parrot**, of which there are perhaps less than 150 left. A few unusual reptiles are also found, including the bright green **Praslin gecko**, the non-poisonous **wolf snake**, the **tiger chameleon**, and a number of different **frogs**.

The main attraction, however, is the coco de mer. As you walk into the forest, the silence is overwhelming.

▼ *Below: Deep inside the emerald-tinged Vallée de Mai forest.*

PARROT OF THE PALMS

The black parrot (*kato nwar*) is actually coffee-coloured, but its legs are black. It whistles in a way that sounds exactly like a street kid, and mynah birds imitate it perfectly as it flies through the jungle of coco de mer palms in the Vallée de Mai. Although secretive and difficult to see, a flock of 30 are sometimes spotted in flight. It climbs with claw and beak and sometimes swings upside down from a male coco de mer catkin. A great fruit eater, it munches into anything from mangoes to figs or the bitter *bilinbi*. The latest count indicates that there are only 150 of these birds left in the world, being cared for almost full time by a Conservation Officer.

Above and close around are the phalanxes of monstrous palms, soaring 30m (100ft) to a sombre canopy of knife-pleated fronds the width of a room, with clusters of nuts weighing up to 20kg (44lb) each. When a light breeze disturbs one of the looming trees, it fidgets and rasps its fronds against a neighbour, while a gust of wind will send the huge trees into a frenzy of clattering branches which sound like coconuts in a storm falling on a tin roof. Then, just as suddenly as it started, the great giants will rest again, reforming their eerie atmosphere of swirling, sunlight-pierced green light.

Ever since the coco de mer made its first, mysterious appearances around the fringes of the Indian Ocean, it has been the source of legend, wonder and erotic delight. The nut which grows on the shorter female tree looks like a gigantic green acorn, but husked, the black, hard-shelled double coconut strikes a remarkable resemblance to a woman's rounded bottom, while the 1m (3ft) long catkin, covered in yellow flowers, provides the male biological adjunct. Understandably believed to have aphrodisiacal and medicinal powers, the fabled nut commanded fortunes from princes and potentates around India and the Middle East. Sailors knew the coco de mer palm as the tree that emerged from the ocean and provided a nest for the mythical giant *rukh*, or roc, which had a 50m (150ft) wingspan and would carry off any unwary seamen who came too close. The Japanese considered the nut sacred, Indian princes fashioned them into jewelled drinking gourds, and one was even priced at 4000 golden florins.

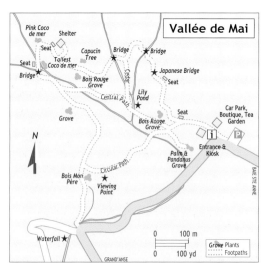

It was not long before the coco de mer aroused interest in a totally different way. General (at that time Colonel) 'Chinese' Gordon visited Praslin in 1881 and wrote a lengthy dissertation entitled *Eden and Its Two Sacramental Trees*. The breadfruit, he decided, was the Tree of Life, while the coco de mer was the Tree of Good and Evil. At a time when the theory of evolution was being hotly debated and Darwin excoriated, Gordon (like today's 'Intelligent Design' fundamentalists in America) believed in a literal interpretation of the Bible. He colourfully explained the Book of Genesis in terms of Praslin, the Vallée de Mai and the coco de mer palm. This explanation may not have found its way into mainstream theology, but nevertheless his theories were to become the pivotal drawcard of Seychelles tourism: the scented Garden of Eden, God's tropical paradise among the palms, islands of love a thousand miles from anywhere in the far Indian Ocean. And few can deny the effectiveness of the image.

▲ *Above: The long, flower-speckled catkin on a male coco de mer palm.*

Praslin Island Walks

Praslin is small enough to ensure that cycling and walking are each an excellent way to get to know the island. There is not much traffic, it is relatively flat around much of the coastline, and there are plenty of quiet paths leading through old plantations and out to windswept viewpoints. Buses (with fares less than US$1) run regularly around the coastal road, so it is never difficult to get back to your hotel.

BLACK PEARLS

Smaller than the coco de mer but even more valuable is the Seychelles black pearl. These gorgeous droplets are cultivated at the aquaculture farm near Amitié airport. Known to the Chinese as the 'secret soul' of the oyster, pearls were first 'cultured' in 1896. Black pearls can be copper, gold or silvery blue and a trophy string can set you back US$200,000.

DUFRESNE

Chevalier Marion Dufresne, the man who claimed Praslin for France in 1768, was a man who had an eye for historic moments. Twelve years earlier he had picked up Bonnie Prince Charlie off the Scottish coast after the Young Pretender had been defeated by the English at Culloden. Dufresne is supposed to have buried a deed of claim at Anse Possession, and, needless to say, people have been trying to find it ever since.

▼ *Below: The round Praslin country road goes past sleepy Anse Marie-Louise, a delightful spot for handline fishing.*

Anse Possession: Leaving from **St Matthew's Church** in Grand'Anse, the narrow road passes the attractive Britannia Hotel and leads up into breadfruit tree patches scattered with rock-perched houses. At the saddle of the hill 140m up you can look out over the ocean to Mahé. From here the right-hand road heads towards Salazie and Côte d'Or, while the left-hand road follows the **Pasquiere River** down to Anse Possession, site of Dufresne's first landing, on the edge of **Curieuse Island Marine Park**.

Southern Tip: Another route is to go south out of Grand'Anse, carry on past the turning to Vallée de Mai, and walk along the coast road as waves crash against the sea wall at high tide, spray almost touching the palm fronds. Past the elegant Coco de Mer Hotel, where you might see a black parrot, there is a collection of delightful pocket-sized coves – **Cemetery**, **Boat**, **Consolation** and the larger **Marie-Louise** – each with high-rise cliffs. **Pointe Cocos** is the southernmost tip of Praslin Island; from here it is not too far over to **Baie Ste Anne**.

◀ *Left: Ocean rollers dashing against spectacular granite boulders frame the powder sands of Anse Lazio in Baie Chevalier.*

Baie Chevalier: One of the most pleasant walks (especially early in the morning) is to go north to Baie Chevalier. From Grand'Anse you walk past the new airport buildings at **Amitié** and the Black Pearl's giant clam breeding aquarium. **Cousin** and **Cousine** islands, the enchanting siblings of North Praslin, are 2km (1.2 miles) off the almost blinding snow-white beach. Near the end of the road there is a turn-off to the new Lémuria Resort which has unfortunately managed to cordon off three of the loveliest beaches on Praslin – Anse Kerlan, Petite Kerlan and Anse Georgette – to give exclusivity to its 18-hole golf course. (Do not be fooled by resort hotel regulations; everyone is allowed on any beach in Mahé, Praslin and La Digue – otherwise guests would presumably be confined to their resorts.) **Pointe Ste Marie** overlooks **Anse Kerlan**. A white handmade cross stands at St Marie's Point offshore of the resort in memory of a child who drowned here many years ago.

A path then leads over the red earth hills covered in latanier palms and pandanus until it reaches the deep blue water and white curve of sand at Baie Chevalier, the quintessential pirate cove. Deep and reef-free, it is a popular yacht anchorage, and boasts a good restaurant revelling in the name of Bonbon Plume. From the restaurant a rough road proceeds to **Anse Boudin**,

PRASLIN

▶ *Right: Anse Lazio beach, voted one of the world's most beautiful.*

where the round-Praslin buses start up again. Or you could go up the mountain to Grand Fond viewsite.

CURIEUSE

Curieuse Island, a kilometre off the northern coast of Praslin, lies within the Marine Park. The area is home to both fish and coral of every extraordinary variety and colour; snorkelling or diving in the clear, warm water is to feast on the silent wonder of the living reef.

The garden under the sea is every bit as exotic as that on Curieuse behind. Rounded brain corals, stag corals, spiky black sea urchins, giant cowries, purple-lipped clams, and thousands of darting, flashing fish can all be seen. There are blushing brown octopus, razor-toothed barracuda, moray eels darting from their caverns, batfish, lovely blue and yellow surgeonfish, big horned and drowsy Picasso triggerfish, and the needle-thin trumpet fish. Loveliest of all is the dappled brown hawksbill turtle, winging away in the blue. Many flipper up onto the beautiful white beach facing Praslin each year to lay their eggs. The park contains an abandoned turtle pond at Baie Laraie built 90 years ago but its muddy mangrove waters enclosed by a 500m (550yd) causeway across the mouth of the bay didn't meet the approval of the turtles.

The island, 3.5km (2 miles) long, named in 1768 by Lieutenant Lampériaire, Captain of the schooner *La Curieuse*, is a breeding centre for 250 giant tortoises, coco de mer palms and black parrots. It was originally called Île Rouge, its distinctive red soils laid bare by repeated fires. From 1833, Curieuse was a leprosy village – initially for sufferers and slaves released from Mauritius – until the discovery of the breakthrough drug Dapsone in the 1960s made it redundant. The ruins of the 1930s village can still be seen at Anse St José as well as the lovely *takamaka*-shaded double-storey Doctor's House built by Sir William MacGregor, the 26-year-old Scottish physician who came to Curieuse in 1873. His home is now a museum and national monument. There are good walking trails round the island. The one that leads from the baby tortoise pens to Anse Badamier on the east coast, a well-forested area, will also enable you to branch off to 172m (564ft) Curieuse Peak. Trees on the trails are tagged and numbered, including the indigenous *calice du pape* and *bwa rouz* screw pine.

PRASLIN FEAST

A special Seychelles menu to get your mouth watering:

Stuffed *palourde* clams

•

Tek tek soup with a drop of Takamaka Bay rum

•

Coétivy crayfish with *citrons*

•

Poached jobfish *à la mode* with parsley

•

Octopus curry in coconut cream, served with rice, mango and grated shark satini, pawpaw, *frisiter* (prickly pear), lentils, eggplant and mixed vegetable pickle hashard. With *palmiste* millionaire's salad

•

Stewed and lightly chilled *frisiter* and Karambol fruit compote

•

Thé du Citronelle

◀ *Left: At Anse Bois de Rose, Coco de Mer Hotel's jetty leads to a mid-sea pergola and bar.*

Rice pudding, Vanilla Napoleons, Bird's Custard and of course vanilla ice cream all go back to the ancient Aztecs of Mexico who loved a hint of vanilla in their hot chocolate, a delight shared by the Spanish *conquistadores* who brought the *vaina* pod to Europe. Seychelles has been growing the *Vanilla planifolia* vines since 1868 and by 1900 was exporting more than all Britain's colonies combined. Coca Cola is the world's largest consumer, while Rochas and Dior use it in their perfumes. The Seychelles wild orchid or *lavannir maron* produces gorgeous white flowers but no vanillin.

COUSIN

Cousin Island, lying 2km (1 mile) from Praslin's Anse Kerlan beach, is a little island covered in indigenous *mapou* and *bwa torti* forest, and a designated Special Reserve. It was purchased by Birdlife International in 1968 and is now administered by **Nature Seychelles** to protect its endangered and rare birds, particularly the **Magpie Robin** and **Seychelles brush warbler** (*le petit merle des îles* in French). Only rangers live on this island and only 20 people at a time may visit.

Breeding **shearwaters**, large brown birds that bank low over the water between the waves, are protected on Cousin. Sometimes you can see 'rafts' of as many as a thousand sitting on the water fishing for squid or flying fish, returning to their nests in the evening moaning and groaning. White **fairy terns** with little blue-black beaks, **tropicbirds**, the little **yellow-capped fody** or *tok tok* (from the sound of its cry), and Seychelles blue pigeons are all common on Cousin. There are also 100,000 breeding **lesser noddies**, and the population of **warblers** has increased from only 26 left in the world to today's several hundred.

Hawksbill turtles come to lay their eggs on Cousin's beaches from August to April. They are the subject of the world's longest-running intensive monitoring programme of this species, with constant observation.

▶ *Right: A solitary* veloutier *bush creeps towards the sea.*

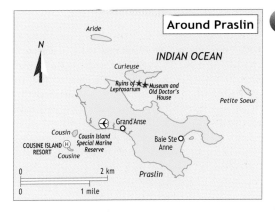

Around Praslin

Aride

N

INDIAN OCEAN

Curieuse

Ruins of ★ Museum and
Leprosarium Old Doctor's
House

Petite Soeur

Grand'Anse

Cousin
Cousin Island
COUSINE ISLAND (H) Special Marine
RESORT Reserve
Cousine

Baie Ste
Anne

0   2 km

0   1 mile

Praslin

COUSINE PRIVATE NATURE RESERVE

'Hold tight,' the skipper calls as he turns the open boat towards the waves and beach. 'Just like the Quantum of James Bond.' And you roar through the pass and up onto the powdery white beach of tiny Cousine Island, truly a one-man-saved Garden of Eden.

Cousine's four villas, possibly the most luxurious of Seychelles' bevy of glamorous resorts, are not there to make money. Every cent spent on Cousine stays on Cousine to finance the granitic island – a dedicated nature reserve, a haven of conservation. There are 21 giant tortoises (three types altogether in Seychelles), each named (MacGregor, Gertrude, Junior), a host of breeding hawksbill sea turtles, the vulnerable Seychelles wolf snake (non-toxic), Wright's endemic skink, the green-day gecko, five species of butterflies, 20 types of ant, four different ghost crabs, and a continuous swirl of endemic birds including impish fairy terns, Seychelles warbler, Seychelles magpie robin, white eye, blue pigeon, nine species of tern sea birds, turtle doves, fody, sunbirds, shearwaters, noddies, frigate birds, crab plovers, curlews, sandpipers, and a list of 40 visitors and vagrants that pass by for a drink.

Nesting hawksbill turtles *(Eretmochelys Imbricata)* are are a feature of the island's pristine scimitar-shaped egg-laying beach and a priority for the island's resident

▲ *Above: The gravel road over to Praslin's Baie Chevalier looks out to Aride Island.*

conservationists – a husband-and-wife team from South Africa. Millipedes are the star workers. Reaching a foot in length, they consume 17% of all available leaf litter on the island each day, forming a rich natural fertilizer and performing a vital function in soil production and nutrient cycling.

ARIDE

From banks of beautiful reefs and a tiara of white sand, Aride Island, 10km (6 miles) north of Praslin, rises in luxuriant guano-fed vegetation to a lovely plateau. It is a long green island of unbelievable beauty, which has been preserved from the planter's axe ever since it was first visited by man in 1756. The old Seychellois family Chenard owned it for 100 years and insisted it became a protected Seychelles sanctuary, which it soon did when purchased in 1973 by Christopher Cadbury of the chocolate family, and it is run today by Seychelles' Island Conservation Society.

Aride, even more so than Cousin, is Seychelles' great bird paradise. Only Aldabra boasts more varieties of breeding sea bird, and between May and October over a million birds lay their eggs on the island. It is home to more **lesser noddies** than anywhere else in the world, an unusual hilltop **sooty tern** colony (360,000 pairs) and a total of 10 species of breeding sea birds. Among the granitic islands, only Aride plays host to breeding **red-tailed tropicbirds**. There are also big populations of **white-tailed tropicbirds**, **fairy terns**, **shearwaters** and the huge, stealth-bomber **frigate birds**.

The English artist and botanist Marianne North, who came exploring the Seychelles in the 1880s, visited Aride to paint **Dr Wright's gardenia**. Known as *bwa sitron* in Kreol (it looks like a lemon), this shrub has a heavenly scent, trumpet-shaped white flowers flecked with magenta, and a hard round green fruit. Some 2000 still grow on Aride, but nowhere else on earth.

Aride is one of the most memorable islands in Seychelles. Visits (Sunday, Monday, Wednesday) to the island are controlled both by the warden and the weather, which can make landing difficult.

Aride's protected habitat has been a tremendous boon to Seychelles' endangered wildlife and plant species, particularly the four critically endangered endemic birds of Seychelles (*see* panel, page 94). Meanwhile, Aride's indigenous vegetation has taken on a new life with the cutting down of exotic fruit trees and coconut palms.

◄ *Left: A hawksbill turtle on Cousin Island, where they are monitored and protected.*

> ### Coconut Supreme
>
> There are two million coconut trees in Seychelles.
> • The nut is eaten, squeezed into a cream, or even grilled as a cocktail snack.
> • Perfume, margarine, soap and sunscreens contain coconut oil.
> • The brittle shell, ground and turned into a charcoal paste, lubricates aircraft bearings.
> • Mattresses, anchor ropes, and car seats all benefit from coconut husk coir.
> • Mahé matrons in pre-Dyson days used to polish floors with a half husk underfoot and a flick of the hip.
> • Seychelles shopping bags, heart-shaped fans and roof thatch all make use of the strong fronds.
> • Tasty dainties include heart of palm salad, sweet germinating nut, and coco water.
> • The sap of the tree, toddy or *calou*, tastes like ginger beer. Leave it 12 hours and it will blow your head off.
> • Coconut palm fronds serve as makeshift sails and beach picnic cloths.
> • Coconut root is said to cure many ailments
> • *Poonac*, animal feed from the residue of oil extraction.
> • Split husks are used to grill whole breadfruit, or as swimming floats for kids.
> • *Tammy* is woven into hats, sunshades and cooking filters.

BEST TIMES TO VISIT

December to **February** are rainy. It can pour down, but rainfall on Praslin is slightly lower than on Mahé. Temperatures remain fairly constant at 30°C (86°F) and humidity 80%. At night the temperature drops a few degrees. There's always a breeze of 6 to 7 knots increasing to 12 knots and more in **June** through **September**, the sailing season.

GETTING THERE

The quickest way is by Air Seychelles (daily flights every 15 minutes 06:00–18:15, later on weekends, tel: 248 381300 or 381000); the adventurous way by schooner (Schooners Praslin, tel: 248 232329); and the expensive way by Cat Cocos ferry (tel: 248 324843), from the inter-island quay off Independence Ave. Helicopter Seychelles shuttle, tel: 248 385863. Mason's Travel offers regular transfers on their luxury launch *Le Cerf*, tel: 248 288888. Arrive at both the airport or the Inter Island Quay at least 30 minutes beforehand.

GETTING AROUND

There are comfortable *Tata* **buses** that circle the island every 45 minutes. Both sides of Praslin are relatively flat, and **bicycles** can be hired from Côte d'Or and Grand'Anse or borrowed from your guesthouse. There are **taxis** at both airport and jetty. For **car hire** try Grand Bleu, tel: 248 293960. But the best way to see Praslin is to **walk**.

WHERE TO STAY

Some small hotels are more luxurious than the large hotels.

SMALL HOTELS

Hotel du Café des Arts, Côte d'Or beach, tel: 248 232170, e-mail: café@seychelles.net website: www.cafe.sc Six rooms. Step out to breakfast on the beach. Owned by artist Christine Harter (*see page 78*).
Amitie Chalets, Amitie Beach, tel: 248 233216, e-mail: martini@seychelles.net web: www.the-seychelles.com Four rooms.

MID-RANGE

Indian Ocean Lodge, Grand'Anse, tel: 248 233324, e-mail: iol@seychelles.net website: www.indianocean lodge.com 32 rooms; beach pool, pub and restaurant. Lots of character. Recommended.
Hotel Coco de Mer and **Black Parrot Suites**, Anse Bois de Rose, tel: 248 290555, e-mail: cocodem@seychelles.net website: www.cocodemer.com 52 rooms. There's always a warm welcome at this palm-fringed hotel. Excellent cuisine.
Village du Pêrcheurs, Côte d'Or beach, tel: 248 290300, e-mail: village@seychelles.net web: www.thesunsethotel group.com Smart boutique hotel.
Le Duc de Praslin, Anse Volbert near Côte d'Or beach, tel: 248 294800, e-mail: leduc@seychelles.net 24 rooms; another great hotel on Côte d'Or's strip.

Le Relax Beach Resort, Grand'Anse, tel: 248 233238, e-mail: beachresort@lerelax hotel.com www.lerelaxhotel. com 10 rooms. Island views.

TOP DOLLAR

Acajou, Côte d'Or, tel: 248 232400, e-mail: acajou@ seychelles.net website: www.acajouhotel.com Built entirely of mahogany. Double storey around pool, 28 rooms.
Hotel l'Archipel, Anse Government, tel: 248 284700, e-mail: archipel@seychelles.net website: www.larchipel.com 30 rooms, tropical hillside garden setting. Complimentary windsurfing.
Paradise Sun, Côte d'Or, tel: 248 293293, e-mail: paradise@seychelles.net website: www.paradisesun.com 80 chalets, range of facilities. Idyllic beach location.
La Reserve, Anse Petite Cour, flanking Curieuse Marine Park, tel: 248 298000, e-mail: resa@lareserve.sc website: www.lareserve.sc 32 rooms (16 bungalows), candle-lit jetty and swim-up bar.
Raffles, Takamaka Bay, tel: 248 429 6780, e-mail: praslin@raffles.com website: www.raffles.com/ praslin 86 hillide villas.

BUDGET

Beach Villa, beachfront Grand'Anse, tel: 248 233445, e-mail: martin@seychelles.net Nine rooms, ask for room 9. Great sunsets. Recommended.

Islander's Guesthouse, Anse Kerlan, tel: 248 233224, e-mail: islander@seychelles.net Self-catering. Eight rooms. Beach was location for film *Castaway*. Near Lémuria golf course.

Britannia, Grand'Anse village, tel: 248 233215, e-mail: britannia@seychelles.net website: www.seychelles.resa.com 12 rooms, excellent Kreol food.

Îles des Palmes, Anse Takamaka (N.E.), tel: 248 232941, e-mail: islands@seychelles.net website: www.beachbungalow.sc 18 bungalows, all on beach.

Cousine Island
Cousine has only four villas, a sanctuary of silence for the turtles and sea birds as well as their guests. Just off Praslin, tel: 248 321107, e-mail: cousine@seychelles.net, website: www.cousineisland.com Recommended.

WHERE TO EAT

Hotels and guesthouses have restaurants. Also worth trying:
Café des Arts on Côte d'Or beach, tel: 248 232131/70. Excellent cuisine, art gallery and beach setting.

Bonbon Plume, Anse Lazio north coast, tel: 248 232136. On exquisite powdery beach. Usually only serves lunches.

Black Parrot, Grosse Roche, tel: 248 233034. Some say this is the best restaurant in Praslin. The first restaurant on the island (50 years ago) was also called the Black Parrot.

La Goulue Café, Côte d'Or, tel: 248 232223. Spicy fish curries.

Capricorn Restaurant, Anse Kerlan, tel: 248 233224. Closed Sun. Beach barbecues. Meals at 'satisfying prices'.

Indian Ocean Lodge, Grand'Anse, tel: 248 233324. Good value Kreol cuisine.

Britannia Restaurant, Grand'Anse, tel: 248 233215. Small established Kreol restaurant. Nice atmosphere.

Airport Touchdown Restaurant, Amitié, tel: 248 233655. Serves snacks.

TOURS AND EXCURSIONS

Local tour operators offer many options. Check with your hotel.
Bird-watching. Three-hour trips to Cousin Island bird sanctuary from Maison Des Palmes Hotel, Grand'Anse. Tues–Fri, 09:30–12:00 and 14:00–16:00. Not open holidays. No restaurant, no overnight, no swimming, no smoking, lots of mozzies.
Curieuse Marine Park. Day boat trips with lunch can be organized through any hotel or tour operator. With a snorkelling stop at St Pierre Islet.
Diving (and learning to dive). PADI courses, night dives, and wonderful coral and sea life in Curieuse Marine Park; 8 dive centers on Praslin, try Octopus, Côte d'Or, tel: 248 232350.

Water Sports. Catamaran sailing, hobie cats, paddle skis, windsurfers, etc. Particularly Côte d'Or. Some hotels have their own equipment.
Vallée de Mai National Park. Tour operators undertake tours around the home of the coco de mer. Or, take a taxi or bus, get a map with your entrance fee and do it yourself. **Golf** at Lemuria's 18-hole golf course.
Bus. Catch one, take a picnic to the cove of your choice.
Cousin Island Sanctuary. Check with your hotel for weekday boat sightseeing, e.g. *Papillon*. **Tours from Mahé**. Tour operators' day trips to Praslin include hotel pickups, air or sea cruise transfers, and transport to Vallée de Mai, Curieuse Marine Park, Cousin, or Aride Island. Other tours combine Praslin and La Digue.

USEFUL CONTACTS

Air Seychelles: tel: 248 284666. **Tourist Office**: tel: 248 233346 (airport). **Health**: Clinic at Grand'Anse, small hospital at Baie Ste Anne, tel: 248 232333. **Tour Operators**: Mason's Travel, tel: 248 288750, or Creole Travel Services, tel: 248 233223. **Emergency**: 999.

PRASLIN	J	F	M	A	M	J	J	A	S	O	N	D
AVERAGE TEMP. °F	81	82	82	82	82	81	79	79	79	81	81	79
AVERAGE TEMP. °C	27	27.5	28	28	28	27	26	26	26.5	27	27	26.5
SEA TEMP. °F	82	80	82	80	78	77	73	73	73	79	77	80
SEA TEMP. °C	28	27	28	27	26	25	23	23	23	26	25	27
RAINFALL in	12	7	6	5	5	4	2	4	5	6	7	12
RAINFALL mm	295	172	160	124	135	116	53	99	130	141	179	311
Days of Rainfall	9	5	6	6	6	3	3	4	4	5	5	10

5
La Digue

La Digue is chunky and different. Named after one of the French expeditionary sailing ships of 1768, the 2000 or so La Digueois would like to consider their island a separate republic. Here they travel in oxcarts on newly paved, sometimes sand roads, there is no airport (although there is a helipad), they rely on ferries and schooners to connect with the rest of the world, men go shirtless and shoeless, and even the Kreol language can be different.

La Digue, the fourth largest of the granitic islands, yet only 5km (3 miles) by 3km (2 miles) at its widest, lies a short schooner sail from Praslin's Baie Ste Anne. It is still the most traditional of the islands, although that and the addictive rural atmosphere does make it increasingly attractive to visitors. There are 23 hotels and guesthouses on La Digue, and it is well within range for day trips from Praslin, yet tourists are still barely apparent. Once on the island there is nowhere more than an hour's walk away, although oxcarts and bicycles (with supermarket shopping baskets) are used to get about. Only a few cars and a couple of minibuses disturb the strolling, bicycling inhabitants of the island.

La Digue is dominated by the 333m (1093ft) **Eagle's Nest** mountain and a broad, and at times marshy, agricultural plain on the northern side where most of the small population lives. The island has spectacular black granite boulder formations, particularly along the beaches, curving and grooved as if by the hand of a giant sculptor. At times they can appear almost pink in colour. The beaches, inevitably, are wild, lonely,

CLIMATE

La Digue can be very **wet** in December and January, and on the low-lying marshy plateau the mosquitoes (non-malarial) can be infuriating. It is **windy** from April to September in the south-easterly trade winds, the drier and more comfortable period. **Humidity** is 80% and **daytime temperatures** around 26°C (80°F). The best snorkelling and fishing times are from October to March.

◀ *Opposite: La Digue at sunset, with Praslin in the distance.*

DON'T MISS

*** The schooner sail from Praslin – the first hint of traditional La Digue.

*** A ride in an oxcart. They're normally waiting at the schooner jetty.

** Walks to Grand'Anse, and around the island.

** A fishing trip on a small local boat.

** Cousin Island – bird and turtle reserve.

** Aride Island with its incredible bird life and vegetation.

* La Veuve Paradise Flycatcher Reserve. Walk through the marshlands and past the lily ponds.

* Château St Cloud, and its tortoise pen. Stay for supper.

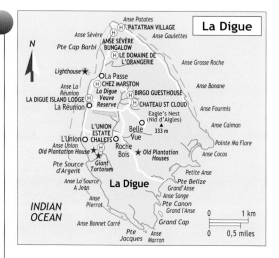

La Digue

SCHOONERS

Sailing has always been a part of Seychelles, from the Arabs in their dhows, who were the first to record the islands, to the age of pirates and naval rivalry. Today it lives on in a very practical way, as the ferries that run between Mahé, Praslin and La Digue are often schooners. When the breeze pipes up it can be exhilarating, with the sails straining and the crew grinning broadly in their yellow oilskins. However, for those not so comfortable with the prospect, the trip from Baie Ste Anne, Praslin, to La Digue can be done by catamaran.

and beautiful, and in **La Digue Veuve Reserve**, the last known habitat of the black paradise flycatcher, there is more evidence of Seychelles' incredible natural heritage. With a cat's cradle of tangled palms and *takamakas* leaning madcap over every gorgeous beach, colourful old tin houses, white waves dashing against granite boulders, and haunting sunsets, it is also the prime destination for fashion magazines, photographers and movie men. *Robinson Crusoe* was one of several films shot on La Digue.

La Digue is one of ten granitic islands grouped around Praslin. **Félicité**, to the northeast of La Digue, has a lodge located on its largest beach, but no other habitation. It was the island where the Sultan of Perak was exiled in 1877. The other islands near Praslin are largely uninhabited, although two, **Cousin** and **Aride**, are fascinating nature reserves, home to some of the rarest and largest of Seychelles' bird populations.

AROUND LA DIGUE

La Passe

La Passe, the main settlement on La Digue, takes its name from the one gap in the island's encircling reef which the schooners from Praslin use to get to the coral pier. In among the palms and *takamakas* arching over the road, which flanks Anse La Réunion beach south of the pier, are several colourful landmarks including Tarosa Café, the library, Chez Marston restaurant, and Gregoire's Supermarket, which apparently has so many more goodies than Mahé shops, that it has bequeathed La Digue with a new laconic nickname: Dubai. A little further on you reach La Digue Island Lodge, one of two sizeable hotels on the island, then the handsome 1854 Assomption church and the turnoff to La Digue Paradise Flycatcher Reserve. The wide road ends at L'Union Estate which has the largest vanilla plantation left in Seychelles. The atmosphere is so unhurried it is difficult to believe much has changed since the first inhabitants, political exiles from the island of Réunion (near Mauritius), settled here and whose old graves can be seen in the cemetery at Cap Barbi.

Behind La Passe, visitors can find one of the real La Digue experiences in **Château St Cloud**, the old St Ange family house overlooking Eagle's Nest mountain. It is a 90-minute walk from the Château up the Belle Vue road to the summit of the island, **Nid d'Aigles** (which means Eagle's Nest, although there have never been any eagles in Seychelles).

Grand'Anse

A road crosses the island from the estate at L'Union to La Digue's version of Grand'Anse, and it is a popular walk. The flat lands are full of the island's traditional air, with the occasional single cow being led out to graze, an old plantation house at the end of a long avenue of palms, all rusting grey tin and decaying arrogance, and such non-Dubai enter-

▼ *Below: Patatran Village Hotel overlooks lovely Félicité Island.*

▲ *Above: Arab, Indian, African, European and Malagasy blend perfectly in the Seychelles people.*

LILY OF THE ISLES

White, magenta and magnificent, the Seychelles lily, or in Kreol *lis dipei* (from the French: *lis du pays*) is probably the most beautiful of the many gorgeous and colourful Seychelles flowers. Its white petals with pink centre stripe grow in clusters of up to 20 trumpet-shaped flowers about 10cm (4 in) in size. You'll often see it in gardens or near the sea when walking about, particularly on the seashore of the smaller islands and La Digue. Long evergreen leaves provide a bouquet for the flowers on their 61cm (2ft) high stalk.

prises as Villa Mon Rêve guesthouse, Monica's Trading Store and Agnes' hair salon. On La Digue you are more likely to see the old plantation equipment and skills (such as rapid-fire husking of coconuts on a stake in the ground) than anywhere else. Despite the increase in tourism, traditional industries such as patchouli, vanilla, copra, saffron, boat building and fishing are still very much a part of La Digue's way of life.

A huge old casuarina tree surrounded by grass and green *veloutier* bush stands sentinel on Grand'Anse, framed at either end by massive pinkish-black, grooved granite boulders. The beach faces the blustering southeast trades, and looks out towards Frégate Island, a blue silhouette in the ocean.

Apart from the ghost crabs scurrying in the foaming surf there may only be a few pairs of wheeling fairy terns, a long-beaked turnstone, or a whimbrel, which migrates 10,000km (6200 miles) from Siberia. Though the sea, without the barrier of the coral reef, seems dramatic and inviting, take note of the multilingual warning sign about the currents.

The East Coast

The track east through the palms goes over a small hill to another equally deserted and beautiful beach, **Petite Anse**, and then on along a series of thundering surf beaches framed by lush forested mountains. La Digue's famous pink granite boulders are strewn around the edges of all these east coast beaches, giving colour both to the sand and the sparkling water lapping around their feet. One of the beaches, **Anse Caiman** (Crocodile Beach), is where the fearsome reptiles basked. By 1777 the first 12 French families and slaves had settled.

At **Anse Fourmis** the island's circular road begins again, weaving in and out of forest, coves, rocky outcrops and deserted beaches. It rounds the northern tip, where the views over the beaches **Anse Gaulettes**, **Anse Patates** (and lovely Patatran Village Hotel) and **Anse Sévère** are a continuous delight, before leading back to La Passe.

Pointe Jacques

South from L'Union beach, a path leads to **Anse Source d'Argent**, epicentre of La Digue's gorgeous beach rock formations, then to **Anse Pierrot** and **Anse Bonnet Carré**, up to Pointe Jacques, the southerly tip of the island, where you will either have to scramble along the shore or over the headland. North from here is a beach, **Grand l'Anse**, with a small island just off it, where the path becomes clearer, and soon joins the main road over the island between Grand'Anse itself and L'Union.

LA DIGUE VEUVE RESERVE

▼ *Below: Dawn reveals sculpted burnt orange rock formations at Grand'Anse beach.*

The plateau on La Digue between the mountain and the sea is dominated by Indian almond (*badamier*) trees, *takamakas* and wetland. The marshes are the habitat of the **Seychelles black paradise flycatcher**, one of the most endangered birds in the world. There are perhaps less than 130 pairs left, all on La Digue. Blueblack from the crown of its head to the tip of its long streamer tail, with a distinctive pale blue bill, the best place to see them is the tiny La Digue Veuve Reserve (*veuve*, or commonly just *vev*, which means 'widow' in Kreol, is the local name for the flycatchers).

The 15ha (37-acre) reserve is not far from Château St Cloud. Set up in a bid to

Seventeen bird species are endemic to Seychelles, but as with many island inhabitants, they are all endangered.
- Seychelles blue pigeon. At a distance it looks like a fish eagle; has a 'ko-ko-kok' cry.
- Seychelles kestrel, or *katiti*, a tiny bird of prey that hides in the eaves of houses.
- Seychelles scops owl, or *syer*. This bare-legged resident of the high mountains is rare and seldom seen.
- Seychelles black paradise flycatcher, known as *vev*, and only found on La Digue. The white, orange and black female is totally different from the long-tailed blue-black of the male.

▶ *Opposite: Château St Cloud, perched below Eagle's Nest mountain.*
▼ *Below: Old schooners still ply the waters of a Digue.*

save an area of natural habitat for the birds, the reserve has an information centre, a nature trail, and a permanent ranger. In the lily pools you might see the pale brown and orange **lily trotter**, or Chinese bittern, stalking across the swamp in search of some tiny bream or frogs. The ranger will also point out the best place to spot the rare **yellow-bellied and star-bellied terrapins**, known as *torti soupap* to the Seychellois, another species sadly endangered by the gradual draining of the marshes. These web-footed reptiles live in freshwater pools and marshes, and eat both plants and snails.

On the road leading down from the reserve to **L'Union** on the coast, there are more lily ponds and mangroves where you might spot some wild orchids. Union Plantation Reserve, with its canopy of soaring, twisted palms, magnificent plantation house (a presidential retreat), old coconut oil mill, copra dryer, and giant tortoise pen is well worth the small entrance fee. The boatyard specializes in making typical Seychellois wooden fishing boats, and *La Bousir* sells snacks and souvenirs.

LA DIGUE ISLANDS

There are four small islands all within a radius of 7km (4 miles) of La Digue: Marianne, Félicité, Grande Soeur and Petite Soeur, plus the La Fouche and Coco islets.

The **Sisters**, to the east of La Digue, are deserted. The larger has two attractive beaches either side of its hourglass middle. There is good fishing all around them, especially for barracuda and wahoo.

Félicité Island

This island, halfway between the two sisters and La Digue, was, for five years in the late 19th century, the home of the exiled

Sultan of Perak. These days isolation carries a healthy price tag, as it is probably the only place in the Seychelles outside the Amirantes where you can hire an island all to yourself. Accommodation has increased but until recently there were only two lovely converted plantation houses, for one group booking only. The fishing is superb, particularly in and around the cluster of islets called Île Cocos.

The island was a plantation run by the Cauvin family for many years and then the favourite holiday spot for presidents and princes. Félicité mountain rises steep above the little hook of beach and chalets, with a path to its 231m (758ft) summit, lush with gnarled old *takamaka* trees and coconuts, and some heart-stopping granite cliffs down to the sea.

Marianne Island

Named after one of the ships which came to Seychelles 200 years ago, Marianne is uninhabited. It is thickly covered in coconuts but conservationists are hoping that the native forest will gradually return. There are some fine rock formations in the south, which can be seen from a boat, that are perhaps even better than La Digue's panoramic sculptures. The darting Seychelles sunbird *kolibri* is there in profusion.

CHÂTEAU ST CLOUD

This 200-year-old, two-storey grey and white stone château – with creaking *takamaka* floors polished with manglier (an extract of mangrove), multi-shuttered windows and only four super-luxury rooms overlooking banks of flowers, breadfruit trees and a giant tortoise pen – would not be out of place in Provence or Blois, the regions of France the St Ange family left to come to Seychelles 200 years ago. In the elegant open dining room Myriam's chefs produce a feast that only island women could devise. Myriam, of Reunion descent and the 16th generation in Seychelles (her father was a government minister), still oversees every detail of the château, often with grandchildren popping in and out of her reception office.

LA DIGUE AT A GLANCE

BEST TIMES TO VISIT

During the **December** to **February** rainy season, the low-lying plateau of La Digue where most of the hotels are sited can be very wet, with some parts flooding. The best times to visit are **April** to **September** when it is less humid and the southeast trades are blowing. Because of its dense forests it always seems more tropical on La Digue. The temperatures, in the main, are the same as the other granitic islands, an average of 27°C (81°F) and 80% humidity.

GETTING THERE

There is no airport on La Digue, but there is a **helipad** at the coast with regular shuttle services. The normal route is to fly by plane to Praslin and take the regular Catrose **catamaran** or **schooner** that normally depart three times a day, and sometimes more frequently, depending on demand. There is one schooner and Le Cerf luxury **fastboat** direct from Mahé. Check days and departure times of all inter-island schooners in Victoria, tel: 248 232329. The faster and more expensive Cat Cocos takes an hour to reach Praslin. Trips to the **smaller islands**, Aride, Curieuse, Cousin, etc., can be arranged through the main Seychelles tour operators including: **Mason's Travel**, tel: 248 288888 (Le Cerf) and 248 234227 (La Digue).

GETTING AROUND

There are now quite a few vehicles on La Digue. Usual transport tends to be oxcart or bicycle. The **oxcarts**, pulled by Brahman bulls, will transport you and your luggage when you arrive at the ferry pier. **Bicycles** can be hired practically anywhere, especially at hotels. There is only one (concrete) road around the island, and only tracks on the **smaller islands** surrounding La Digue (and Praslin), where you will need permission to land. The local manager will probably lend you a bicycle.

WHERE TO STAY

There are 25 mainly small hotels on La Digue. They include:

SMALL HOTELS

Birgo Guesthouse, near Château St Cloud, tel: 248 234518, e-mail: birgo@seychelles.sc, website: www.birgo.sc 12 lovely rooms; B&B only.

TOP DOLLAR

Château St Cloud, inland of Anse La Réunion, tel: 248 234346, e-mail: stcloud@seychelles.net website: www.seychelles.net/stcloud 22 rooms, four in the enchanting old two-storey plantation residence. Run like an elegant country inn at the time of the French Revolution, it also has its own resident giant tortoises.

L'Union Estate Chalets, tel: 248 292525, e-mail: reservation@ladigue.sc This is the most expensive accommodation on La Digue by far. It consists of eight units on an old plantation with a secluded beach. Basically self-catering.

La Digue Island Lodge, Anse Réunion beach, tel: 248 292 525, e-mail: reservation@ladigue.sc 69 thatched A-frames.

Patatran Village, Anse Patates, tel: 248 234333, e-mail: patatran@seychelles.net website: www.patatran seychelles.com Bird's-eye bungalows overlooking ocean and islands. Swimming pool. Recommended.

BUDGET

Chez Marston, tel: 248 234023, e-mail: mars@seychelles.sc With its five new rooms near the jetty, Marston maintains the quixotic 200-year-old St Ange tradition of hospitality.

Anse Sévère Bungalow, North La Digue, tel: 248 247354, e-mail: clemco@seychelles.net One only self-catering beach bungalow, a 10-minute bicycle ride from anyone.

Most small hotels and guesthouses are near La Passe.

ISLANDS

Félicité Island

Félicité has two luxury beach-facing bungalows backed

against dramatic rock formations, for one group booking. Expensive. Contact tel: 248 292525 or 234366, e-mail: reservation@ladigue.sc

Note: there are no accomodation facilities on Marianne and Les Soeurs. A new resort is currently being built on Félicité. However, day visitors can go to any of these islands. Check with tour operators or your hotel.

WHERE TO EAT

Zerof, Anse Reunion, tel: 248 234067. Kreol food. Ring to book.
Le Tournesol, La Passe, tel: 248 234155. Small eatery, great fish curries.
Chez Marston, Anse La Réunion, tel: 248 234023. Good food, and good conversation.
Patatran Village, tel: 248 294300. Deserved reputation for live music and for tasty Kreol food.
Château St Cloud, tel: 248 234346. Elegant French-Kreol cuisine.

TOURS AND EXCURSIONS

Local tour operators on La Digue will assist you with any excursion, hotel booking, bicycle hire or holiday activity. Their offices are all at La Passe jetty as you get off the schooner. As is the Tourist Office, tel: 248 234393, open during office hours.
Helicopter Trips. Shuttle services from Mahé, La Digue,

scenic flights and charters all available. Also to Félicité and Cousine, tel: 248 385863.
Diving. There are at least eight dive centres on Praslin and one on La Digue: Azzura Pro Diving at La Digue Island Lodge, Anse Réunion, tel: 248 234232. Good La Digue dive sites include Anse Marron Bank, Anse Sévère (photography). Surrounding islands' dive sites include: Aride Bank, Wolfgang's Wall (Curieuse) and South Marianne.
Sailing. Hobie cats and windsurfers. Check at the Tourist Office or your hotel.
Fishing. Barracuda, wahoo, tuna, and bonito are plentiful, particularly between Félicité and Les Soeurs, while fishing in a small boat off the reefs is exhilarating. All hotels and guest houses have a favourite fisherman and all can arrange fishing trips.
Rock Climbing. Has not really taken off in Seychelles. If you have you own gear, try Pointe Jacques or Source d'Argent.
Snorkelling. Equipment for snorkelling can usually be borrowed at your hotel.
Horse riding. Short beach rides only at L'Union Estate

as the horses are unshod. C/o La Digue Island Lodge, tel: 248 292525.
Oxcart trips. Inexpensive and available anywhere along the main roads; a leisurely way to see the countryside and meet the villagers.
The **La Digue Festival** takes place on 15 August each year, Assumption Day. It is a grand day with bunting, processions, music, feasting and festivities. It is very popular, attracting folk from Mahé and Praslin, as well as practically all the residents of La Digue.

USEFUL CONTACTS

Air Seychelles, tel: 248 284612 (Praslin).
Telephone Enquiries, tel: 100.
Emergency, tel: 999.
Hospital, tel: 248 234255.
Tourist Office, tel: 248 234393
Mason's Travel, tel: 248 288857
Creole Travel Services, tel: 248 297000, e-mail: info@travelservices.com
Inter-Island Schooners, tel: 248 232329.
La Digue Island Lodge: tel: 248 292525.
Marine Charter (Mahé), tel: 248 322126.

LA DIGUE	J	F	M	A	M	J	J	A	S	O	N	D
AVERAGE TEMP. °F	81	82	82	82	82	81	79	79	79	81	81	79
AVERAGE TEMP. °C	27	27.5	28	28	28	27	26	26	26.5	27	27	26.5
SEA TEMP. °F	82	80	82	80	78	77	73	73	73	79	77	80
SEA TEMP. °C	28	27	28	27	26	25	23	23	23	26	25	27
RAINFALL in	12	6	7	6	5	3	3	6	5	8	6	12
RAINFALL mm	315	149	178	146	129	84	87	124	124	203	154	313
Days of Rainfall	9	5	6	6	5	3	3	3	3	4	5	9

6
A Pattern of Islands

From granite mountains to coral specks, huge atolls to little more than a ring of sand and a solitary palm, the 115 islands of Seychelles stretch like a string of pearls across 1000km (620 miles) of the Indian Ocean. Away from the main island group around Mahé and Praslin, the Seychelles archipelago quickly becomes remote and unknown, yet these Outer Islands are as rich as their more populous siblings, and just as valuable a part of the vivid tapestry of Seychelles.

The vast majority are uninhabited, and visitors common on just a few. To get to some of them is both difficult and adventurous, but for that the rewards seem all the greater. Their names, **Amirantes**, **Alphonse**, **Farquhar** and, possibly the most fascinating of all, **Aldabra**, are ones to conjure up images of wildness and wonder, endless sky, sea and floating islands. They are places where nature is still strongly in command, where unique plants and unusual animals cling to a thin thread of existence, not always threatened by man, but often simply by the wheels of nature itself.

BIRD ISLAND
Bird, the most northerly of the Seychelles islands, is a nugget of coral, palms, turquoise tropical sea, and a million breeding sea birds. Everyone has their favourite island in Seychelles, and for many who have managed to get there only once, this is Bird.

As you get off the Otter aircraft after a half-hour flight from Mahé, the manager is there to greet you and soon

Amirantes Group   Mahé

Alphonse
Group

Aldabra
Group   INDIAN OCEAN

Farquhar Group

CLIMATE

The **rainfall** is higher in the granitic islands of Silhouette, Frégate and around Mahé than in the hotter and drier coral islands like Denis, the Amirantes chain and the great atolls of the south: Aldabra, Cosmoledo and Farquhar. The latter can experience **cyclones** in the northwesterly monsoon from December to February. Very few of the coral islands have the forests of the granitic group but all have shady palms and casuarinas, and as low islands in a wide sea they have refreshing **breezes** whatever the season.

◄ *Opposite: Romantic beaches, romantic islands.*

103

DON'T MISS

★★★ Staying at a remote and luxurious island lodge. The islands become all yours.
★★★ A few days with the birds on Denis or Bird Islands.
★★★ A sail to the Amirantes – each evening a new island.
★★ The thrill of fishing for sailfish and marlin.
★★ A walk on coral mushrooms on Aldabra.
★★ Scuba diving – corals and fish in crystal clear water.
★★ Silhouette's Dauban mountain: lush mist forests and magical untouched flora.
★ Frégate Island: your best chance for pirate treasure.

▶ Opposite: Cool breezes and palm trees surround the bungalows of Bird Island.

over a welcoming fruit drink to explain that the essence of Bird is in what it does not have: no air conditioning, no TV, no telephones in the rooms and no need to lock anything away. Even the bar was made out of East Borneo camphor wood washed ashore one stormy night.

Bird Island was originally called Île aux Vaches, after the dugongs, or sea cows, that early French explorers found here. Although there are no dugongs left, there certainly are birds. The island is an endless whirl of them: **fairy terns**, with blue-black beaks and eyes gleaming out of a cloak of white, perch in cuddling couples in the eaves of your bungalow; grey-brown **noddy terns** dominate the seashore, and between May and October each year 850,000 pairs of chattering, crying and wheeling black-and-white **sooty terns** arrive to breed and sit on their speckled eggs.

Each guest receives a check list which includes the common **crab plover**, **sanderling**, **great frigate** and **wedge-tailed shearwater**. In addition, dedicated ornithologists can hope to see the **black cuckoo**, **broad-billed sandpiper**, **corncrake** and an endless range of migrants and vagrants. Whenever you walk

Seychelles

INDIAN OCEAN

Bird Island
Denis Island
Praslin Aride
North Island La Digue
Amirantes African Banks Silhouette Frégate
Group
Mahé
Rémire
D'Arros St Joseph's Atoll Inner Islands
Desroches
Étoile Poivre Atoll Platte
Boudeuse Marie Louise
Desnoeufs
Alphonse Alphonse
Group Bijoutier
St François Coétivy

Outer Islands

Aldabra Atoll Aldabra
Group Providence Providence Atoll
Picard Malabar St Pierre Bancs Providence
Grande Terre Menai Cosmolédo Atoll Farquhar
Assomption Grand Île Group Farquhar Ridge
Astove Goëlettes Île du Nord
Farquhar Île du Sud
Atoll

N

0   200 km
0   100 miles

on the island there is the cry of sea birds. They nest up trees, on the beach, and even the Lodge is shaped like a giant frigate bird.

Around Bird Island

At the northern sandbank on the island the open flat beach reveals nothing but sooty terns. They dive and hover a metre above you, their masked faces curious and inquisitive. Their nest is a simple open 'scrape' of sand; if you are gentle they will allow you to get quite close. Before the island was declared a wildlife sanctuary in 1986, this placid attitude was exploited by egg collectors. There are six major sooty tern colonies in Seychelles: on Bird, Aride, Desnoeufs, Cosmoledo, Farquhar and Denis.

Bird Island only covers 69ha (170 acres), and at most it takes two hours to walk around its encircling white-on-white beach with smooth grey driftwood sticking up out of the sand. Sky blue waters surround the island which is bounded by jagged reef at **Passe Hirondelle** on the eastern side. Turtles come up on the beaches to lay their eggs, the hawksbill quite often during the day. Everything is carefully recorded.

One friend you'll definitely make is **Esmeralda**, the island's pet tortoise. Weighing in at 298kg (657lb), Esmeralda (she is actually a he) is recorded in the *Guinness Book of Records* as the largest tortoise in the world.

Bird Island

★ Sooty Tern Breeding

★ Anchorage

Passe Hirondelle

Ⓗ BIRD ISLAND LODGE

✈

Passe Cocos

Passe Endormi

0   500 m

0   500 yd

ISLAND FOLK

Georges and Margaret Norah managed Bird Island for years. For them, turtles were not for harpooning, shells were for the seashore and sooty tern eggs were for the birds, not gourmet omelettes. They have seen the island's bird population grow from 20,000 to a million. Breeding hides for tropicbirds were created, Seychelles sunbirds introduced and the beaches have become a haven for egg-laying turtles. They have won conservationist and responsible tourism awards, educated their sons themselves, delivered a baby, reassured an Italian couple that geckos in their chalet were not baby crocodiles, and finally patented a salinity-reduction system for coral atoll wells.

▲ *Above: Blue skies, a million birds and silent seas – Bird Island.*

DENIS ISLAND

Governor Sweet-Escott, doing his round of the islands by boat in 1903, came to Denis, the guano-rich, and hence verdant, coral island 50km (31 miles) east of Bird. There he found that the light-house was 'in capital order and the quarters of the lightkeeper very much improved'. The light-house, refurbished in 1910, is still there but the accommodations have changed out of all recognition. The 25 sumptuous air-conditioned bungalows (inside and outside showers), each with its own private beach and almost invisible from each other, are run by owners Mickey and Kathleen Mason. Their son Alan now runs Mason's Travel while Mickey is successfully developing the agricultural base of Denis. Mason is like Robinson Crusoe in his flair for experimentation. Denis is the only island in Seychelles, other than Mahé, to produce its own fresh milk, and using drip irrigation supplies all Denis' vegetable and fruit needs, as well as those of Praslin's Indian Ocean Lodge. The list includes paw-paws (20 large ones on each tree), jamalaks, bananas, breadfruit, mangoes, golden apples, passionfruit, limes, oranges and, of course, palmiste and coconuts, extract-ing oil from the latter and bottled for sale. The Masons have introduced cattle, pigs, ducks, quails, breeding tor-toises, rabbits and 2000 chickens. One-seventh of the island's 350 acres is being left as original woodland while another area has been cleared to encourage migratory sooty terns to settle and breed. The Masons have replanted thousands of indigenous trees in the lush forests once decimated by guano mining.

Denis was named after sea captain Denis de Trobriand, who anchored off its ring of blue water and

DEEP-SEA FISHING

Game, or fighting fish, such as black marlin, blue marlin, tuna, wahoo, bonito and barracuda, are all found in Seychelles' waters, along with the prince of them all, the sailfish, which features on Seychelles' coat of arms. The best months for sailfish are March to June, October and November. A number of boats are available to charter for fishing, with skippers who know the waters well. Speak to Marine Charter, or head for Denis or Bird's close-in fishing grounds.

snowy beach in his vessel *L'Etoile* on 11 August 1773, en route to India. Sited on the edge of the Seychelles Bank, which disappears into a 2000m (6500ft) abyss, the island has become very popular with deep-sea fishermen as the fishing for marlin and sailfish is always good. Denis has several unusual touches: an abandoned prison, a cemetery, a chapel, and some unusual coastal coral formations known as the Caves.

SILHOUETTE

Silhouette stands as a ghostly, mist-capped pyramid in a silvery sea, a shrouded dark shape against the sunset. It is the island you see from Beau Vallon Bay on Mahé, Seychelles' high-forested answer to Bali Hai in the South Pacific. Only 19km (12 miles) from Mahé, it is the third-largest island in the archipelago, and the only one with mist forests as high as those on Mahé. The highest point is the 740m (2428ft) Mount Dauban. Silhouette gives its name to Air Seychelles' in-flight magazine, but the name of the island in fact came from a French finance comptroller, Etienne de Silhouette, rather than from its moody, darkened profile.

COWRIES

Of the 165 known species of cowrie, a mollusc, 50 can be found in Seychelles.

• Cowries are the homes of living creatures that feed on algae. The fleshy mantle of the animal creates the hard, glossy shell.

• The name originates from the Hindu word *kauri*; the shells have often been used as a form of currency.

• Two of the most common cowries in Seychelles are the Tiger and the Arabian cowrie.

▼ Below: The aquamarine seas and talcum white sands of Denis Island.

Medical doctors, teachers, airline pilots or expatriates with specialist skills may find employment in Seychelles. Crime is negligible, housing plentiful, health care good, there is no malaria and education is excellent. The downside is that the cost of living is considerably higher than in Europe, you need a Gainful Occupation Permit, government salaries can be in rupees only, and tropical life can become 'another bloody day in paradise'. However, if you are an eccentric poet with a private income, all is possible.

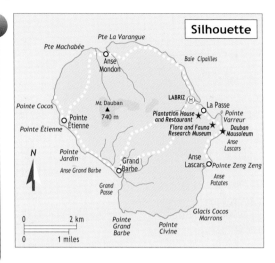

Silhouette was owned for many years by the Dauban family (the double-storey Plantation House is now a restaurant), and has therefore been relatively untouched by both the planter's axe and the developer's foundation stone. Before helicopters and the 52-seater Labriz motor launch that docks to chilled cocktail fruits and champagne, getting to Silhouette was a hazardous affair. Judging the swell and the jagged coral of La Passe was an exercise fraught with danger.

A thousand years ago the island was known to Arab seamen from the East Indies (or *lascars*, as they are called in Seychelles). Graves and ruins at Anse Lascars are believed to be of Arab origin but it will probably take sophisticated archaeological examination to confirm this. Ships of the English East India Company sighted Silhouette in 1609, while 200 years later Le Corsair Hodoul spent some time here. It is claimed (as it is for practically every island in Seychelles) that he buried treasure on one of its beautiful beaches.

Around Silhouette

Silhouette is roughly round in shape, 5km (3miles) long by 4km (2.5 miles) wide, and is completely surrounded

◀ *Left: Often capped in mist, pyramid-peaked Silhouette Island dominates every view from northwest Mahé.*

by reef. Labriz Resort with 110 villas, a fitness centre and spa challenges Silhouette's Forgotten Eden idyll somewhat. Until recently, no money was used on Silhouette and there were only 200 inhabitants, a clinic, a school, and at Anse Grand Barbe, a lovely church.

Mont Dauban mountain is a tropical mist forest crammed with botanical treasure, including the rare pitcher plant with its secret juices which dissolve insects. Tiny orchids and rare hardwoods such as *bwa rouz* and *bois de natte* grow there, while the rare incense tree *bwa sandal* is found only on Silhouette. Other Silhouette specials include the *trilepisium madagascariense*, or false fig tree, discovered in 1883 on Mont Dauban, probably by the indefatigable Marianne North. The Nature Protection Trust of Seychelles (concentrating on tortoises) and the old plantation house are at La Passe. Nearby is a lovely lagoon surrounded by palms and mangroves. High in the lush rocky mountains, on the trail from **La Passe** to **Grand Barbe**, you can see fruit bats hanging from the trees or gliding like prehistoric pterodactyls, the sun catching the leathery sheen of their wings. There are a number of trails on the island, around the rocky coast or up through the thick, mostly untouched high forests.

DAUBAN, QUIXOTE OF SILHOUETTE

Buried in an impressive Grecian-columned mausoleum on Silhouette are generations of Daubans who have owned and run the island since 1864. Auguste Dauban, who fought at Waterloo, was the first to settle here. For much of the 20th century his bachelor descendant Henri Dauban, a tall, gaunt planter, intellectual, and environmentalist, ran Silhouette. A graduate of the London School of Economics, he joined the British Olympic javelin team in 1924, despite the fact that he was a Frenchman. He was an expert pirogue builder and excellent chef. The old family plantation house, built of indigenous hardwoods, still stands at La Passe on Silhouette.

A PATTERN OF ISLANDS

▶ Right: Squabble and scrape, gaggle and haggle – sooty terns by the thousand.
▶▶ Opposite: Frégate Island Hotel gives visitors a floral welcome.

NORTH ISLAND

The first Westerners other than the Portuguese to set foot on Seychelles did so on North Island in 1609 when Englishmen from the *Ascension* landed. Led by Commander Alexander Sharpeigh of the East India Company, the longboats brought back the giant tortoises to eat that John Jourdain, whose diary records the islands for the first time, claimed looked 'soe uglie before they were boyled'.

Tiny North Island is today a castaway retreat for the platinum wristband set. You could purchase Seychelles' annual production of cinnamon bark for a 16-night stay at the smartest of the eleven villas, with personal butler, plunge pool, massage bed, hot and cold running chefs, and organic (naturally) veggies. Don't feel bad: the lodge guarantees all is eco-friendly and in harmony with nature. **Grand Paloss** mountain (214m; 702ft) dominates North Island while paths lead to the plant nursery (with 70+ species) and four beaches including **Cimitière** (Cemetery), recalling the days when a child would often die before the men could row a huge hardwood pirogue the 25km (15 miles) of deep swell ocean to Mahé.

FRÉGATE

This lovely island of only 3km² (1.2 sq miles) is the most remote of the dozen granitic and hence mountainous islands that surround Mahé, a distance of 56km (34 miles) to the west. It used to have the only

POACHED EGGS

John Jourdain, sailing on the *Ascension*, and the first European to give a good documentation of Seychelles, recorded that there were many sooty terns on the islands, 'so tame they could be captured by the dozen'. Their eggs are still collected in the Amirantes for gourmets in Mahé, where a pink-egg omelette is a delicacy. From Desnoeufs (which means eggs), and its surrounding islands, 100 tonnes of egg yolk were exported in 1931, a mere 11 million eggs' worth.

game on Seychelles – Asiatic deer imported from Mauritius. Its main exports since it was first explored in 1744 by French surveyor Lazare Picault have always been rum, copra, cashew nuts, vegetables and above all, the hint of pirate treasure.

Unlike Silhouette, North, or even La Digue, it has an airstrip and there is an elegant one-couple-one-villa-with-a-view lodge on airy cliffs overlooking blue seas. The old plantation house is now one of two restaurants offering fine Kreol cuisine. The ambience is Balinese, the luxury sybaritic and the *objets d'art* could only have been collected by someone fond of collectibles. It has jacuzzis, rock spa, aromatherapy and its own marina.

As to buried treasure, me hearties, Frégate comes tantalizingly close to the real thing. The island's first visitors were 18th-century buccaneers seeking refuge from marauding colleagues and the yardarm nooses of French and British men o' war. A sunken well lined with lead, ruins, cannonballs and gold have all apparently been found, and coral tombs have been reported. In 1812 a

CORAL REEF FISH

There are 1000 species of reef fish in Seychelles:
- Parrot fish: bright blending colours. Named after their parrot beaks.
- Razor fish: thin, pencil-like creatures that swim in a vertical handstand position.
- Blue angelfish: a flat, square fish with iridescent blue edging to its wings.
- Moorish idol: gorgeous zebra markings and white top streamer.
- Batfish, or *pouldo* in Kreol. As large as a tennis racquet, they will swim alongside you.

HERCULES

- The Latin name of Frégate's huge tenebrionid beetle is *pulposipes herculeanus*.
- Its Kreol name is *bib arme*, which means armed spider, but despite its knobbly, spidery legs, it is a beetle.
- European entomologists seeing specimens for the first time were convinced that it was a hoax, stuck together from bits of other insects.
- It is found only on Frégate.

cross-belt and shoulder strap were unearthed, while in 1838 one visitor recorded that 'Spanish piastres and other coins called cruzados have been found on the shore … with calm weather one can distinguish, half a mile from land, the debris of a large ship which lies at the bottom of the sea'. Careful research may yet reveal that all these finds are linked to the Arab seamen who crossed the Indian Ocean in their graceful dhows a thousand years ago, a treasure trove for archaeologists at least, if not bounty hunters.

In the hinterland are lovely forests, their luxuriant trees the favourite crawling territory of Frégate's unique **giant tenebrionid beetle**, which looks like a steel-plated version of the African dung beetle.

Birders come to Frégate, with its seven lonely beaches (particularly Victorin, often voted the world's best, an accolade Seychelles beaches seem to swap exclusively among themselves) and promontories of weather-grooved rocks, to spot the once nearly extinct **Seychelles Magpie Robin**. Twelve years ago there were only 22 of these birds left in the world. Now there are over 100 worldwide, half on Frégate. They are tame ground-feeders with a blue sheen and white feather patches that can be seen as they fly. In Frégate it is known as the *'ti santerz'*, or little singer.

▼ *Below: A manta ray glides into the deep blue.*

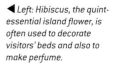

◄ Left: Hibiscus, the quint-essential island flower, is often used to decorate visitors' beds and also to make perfume.

AMIRANTES

'And after some months here we fight, perhaps a bit feebly, against a desire to forget about the world at large.' So wrote New Yorker Wendy Veevers-Carter in 1966 about life on **Rémire Island** in the fabulous Amirantes, a chain of tiny coral atolls covered with palms in the middle of the Indian Ocean. Tragedy struck Veevers-Carter when her husband died on a trip to East Africa; being so remote she only learnt of his death weeks later. Their bungalow, now in ruins, stands facing the pass in the reef on this lovely island, now the occasional retreat of Albert René, the former president.

Rémire is only one in a cavalcade of 25 islands stretching south across 100km (62 miles) of ocean halfway between Mahé and Aldabra. From **Boudeuse** ('the sulky one') to **Marie Louise**, **St Joseph** with its cluster of islets thick with coconut palms, and **D'Arros**, the horizon seems to promise a new island every time you raise anchor. To visit these emerald jewels in a magic sea is an experience that will haunt you forever.

The Amirantes were known to Arab seamen and were named in 1502 in honour of Vasco da Gama (*see* panel, page 113). It takes 24 hours to sail the 250km (155 miles) from Mahé to Rémire, the faint tuft tops of palms being the first warning of land on the horizon. The warning wasn't always heeded, as there

VASCO DA GAMA

Less than a decade after Columbus had reached the West Indies, Portuguese navigator Vasco da Gama set out to find a seaborne route to the East Indies in a bid to break the Arab stronghold on the spice trade. His first voyage in 1497/8 took him round the Cape of Good Hope and up the East African coast – where a Chinese fleet had been 60 years earlier – before crossing to reach the coast of India at Calicut. He was made an admiral (hence 'Amirantes', named after him) just before his second voyage, which took him to Goa, an Indian enclave to become the centre of Portuguese power in the East for the next 500 years.

▲ *Above: A deserted sandy road winds through an old coconut plantation, Desroches.*

PIERRE POIVRE

His name literally translates as Peter Pepper, but perhaps he is more widely remembered as Peter Piper, the man who picked a peck of pickled pepper. A peck was a barrel which had a volume of about 9 litres (2 gallons). He was the first Intendant on the Île de France, the name of Mauritius during French rule. He believed that on both Mauritius and Seychelles he could grow spices to compete with the lucrative trade that was being conducted between the East Indies and Europe.

have been many wrecks in the Amirantes. One of the earliest recorded was that of *HMS Fire* in 1801, after which one Lieutenant Campbell, the commander, successfully sailed to Mahé in a canoe to get help.

Although airstrips have been built on several of the islands, only four are inhabited, and **Desroches** alone has been developed. A luxury lodge (with golf practice range) and a satellite ground station enable this island to lay claim to being 'the doorway to the Amirantes'. Its copra plantation is still working, and timber and charcoal are sent to Mahé. There is a small village of around 50 people while the lodge has 20 chalets and offers some exciting water sports, especially diving and fly bonefishing.

Many islands are not inhabited at all, bar a few adventurous 'Ilois', although at one stage or another most have been exploited for coconuts, green turtle, shark, timber, green snail (mother-of-pearl shells) and, above all, guano. The removal of this dung deposited by tens of millions of birds over thousands of years (particularly during the last ice age when millions of sea birds fled south) has badly affected some islands, leaving them covered with a coral pavement which one has to break through to reach the water table.

The uninhabited 35ha (86-acre) **Desnoeufs**, with a sooty tern colony three times that of Bird Island, was formerly the source of vast quantities of eggs, though now the island is enjoying a degree of protection as a breeding reserve.

Poivre

Poivre, the largest of the Amirantes islands, is named after Pierre Poivre, the man who encouraged the planting of spices in Seychelles. He is to be distinguished from Pierre Poiret, the man who claimed to be the true heir of Marie Antoinette and Louis XVI. Poiret farmed on the island between 1804 and 1822. A long lagoon, rich in bird song and lush vegetation, cuts into the atoll. To pole the length of this lagoon in the early morning, with fairy terns wheeling above the trees, waders strutting, an occasional turtle rising and perhaps even a giant guitarfish wriggling away beneath your boat, can be quite inspiring. At low tide you can walk across the sand from La Pointe to Poivre Island itself, where handsome *bwa blan* trees shade the manager's sparse *La kaz* (cage) house. Accommodation on Poivre is very basic.

ALPHONSE GROUP

The smaller Alphonse group of atolls, three in all, lies 90km (56 miles) further south and 400km (250 miles) from Mahé. **Alphonse** itself is a shovel-shaped island of extraordinary beauty surrounded by perfect coral reef gardens. Small paths circle the island; at either tip, Dot and Tamatave, there are shipwrecks. **Bijoutier**, which means bejewelled, and **St François** complete this cluster. There is now an airstrip and lodge on Alphonse.

▼ *Below: A giant clam nestles menacingly in coral. These clams can be nearly a metre wide and their shells are often used as blessing fonts outside churches in Seychelles. They are farmed on Praslin Island.*

NEW YEAR ON COÉTIVY

Travel writer F.D. Ommaney came to Coétivy at the end of 1947. As they departed on their boat, bonfires had been lit on the shore, he wrote, and the New Year fiesta had begun, while in the little deckhouse cabin '... we drank to 1948 in an old schooner loaded with copra and crawling with inquisitive little beetles. The crew were heaving on the capstan by the glimmer of a lamp on the forestays ... under the first stars of the new year the *Diolinda* spread her dusky wings and slipped into the night'.

▼ *Below: The World Heritage Site plaque at the settlement on Aldabra.*

FAR OUT ISLES

Île Platte (Flat Island) and Coétivy are in the opposite direction to the Amirantes from Mahé, and roughly as far away. **Platte** is renowned for its fishing and broad sandy beaches at either end of its 1.5km (1-mile) length. It seems to emerge as if from nowhere out of a vast expanse of ocean, and many a mariner has come to grief on its reef.

Coétivy covers an area of 931ha (3.5 sq miles), a thin island 10km (6 miles) long and one of the most productive islands both from sea and land in Seychelles. It is from Coétivy that the restaurants of Mahé get their tiger prawns, the delicious *krevet*, a commercially grown prawn which is also exported. Pork, beef, copra, fish, fruit, lamb and an abundance of vegetables are produced on the agriculturally rich soil of Coétivy, something that visitors have noted for years. In 1859 Bishop Vincent Ryan recorded that there were spacious pigsties on the island with 'immense animals in them', while the coconut mill employed 45 donkeys.

The island was first visited by a French sea captain named Coétivy in 1771. The old building ashore has

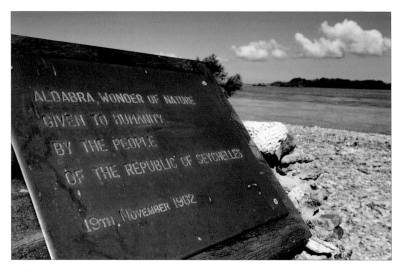

thick walls and doors carved out of heavy *takamaka* wood. Many new buildings have been added to meet the hi-tech agricultural output of this island. Tourists as such do not visit this hard-working, functional island, although the island has both an airstrip and boat landing stage.

ALDABRA

Aldabra, believed to be the world's largest atoll and largest sea lagoon, is made up of a rugged ring of coral tufted with thick scrub. It sits atop a volcanic base and is surrounded by turbulent reef that slides, as if down a mountain slope, into the depths of the sea. Some 34km (21 miles) long and 14.5km (9 miles) across, the land area of the 14 islands around the ring of the atoll is only slightly less than that of Mahé, although its lagoon alone could almost swallow the mountainous main island. It lies 1200km (750 miles) from the granitic islands, and about half that from mainland Africa, a distant, unique sanctuary for ancient animals, flora and marine life.

The shallow **lagoon** is dotted with umbrellas of coral that emerge like mushrooms at low tide to provide landing pads for booby birds. The lagoon, lined with mangroves, empties in a tidal rush every 12 hours through three main passes. At these times it is impossible to make headway in a boat against the turbulence. Yet, in the evening or early morning, and particularly when one of Aldabra's sudden squalls builds up across the lagoon, the shallow water can be a panorama of pastel colours quickly softening the mirror of heat from sea and sky.

Aldabra, rising an unusually high (for a coral island) 8m (26ft) above the navigator's horizon, was named by Arab seamen

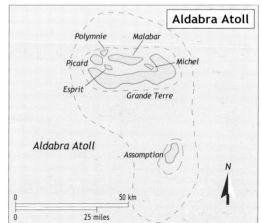

Aldabra Atoll

Polymnie — Malabar
Picard — Michel
Esprit
Grande Terre

Aldabra Atoll

Assomption

N

0   50 km
0   25 miles

MAGIC MUSHROOMS

Aldabra, a limestone coral atoll, was established on a volcanic base which rose from the ocean floor. The limestone has been eroded over the years by rainwater to leave a honeycombed, pitted surface, known as *champignon*, or mushroom. Wave action has also undercut the coral in the lagoon, creating large, mushroom-shaped platforms for birds.

over 1000 years ago. Aldabra could be a version of 'al-khadra', Arabic for the cloud reflecting green off the lagoon, but it could also refer to the heavenly constellation, Aldebaran. In 1964, Aldabra was nearly flattened to build a joint British-US airbase. Conservationists worldwide, alerted by Seychellois leaders, raised the alarm and Aldabra's rare wonderland was saved. Today it is a World Heritage Site and wonder of nature 'given to humanity by the people of Seychelles'.

Flora

Aldabra is no verdant honeymoon isle of silvery sands and whispering palms. Covered in ragged **pemphis scrub**, with the occasional line of **casuarinas** and twisted **palms**, the weather-ravaged surface of the steel grey-coloured coral is like a moonscape of ferociously pitted molten limestone. At the edge of the lagoon the undercut cliffs hang over the water, and when the southeast trades blow, whipping up the water, spray blows up through the holes like angry geysers. Despite the semi-arid, desolate feel, however, the atoll boasts 273 species of flowering shrub and fern, 19 of which grow only on Aldabra and another 22 on only one other island.

Apart from the Aldabra **screw pines** (or *bwa d'amande*) and huge stands of mangroves that line the lagoon, a number of species advertise their rarity with the prefix Aldabra in their name. Two, as if cocking a snoot at their harsh environment with sweet fragrances and delicate flowers, are **Aldabra jasmine** and the **Aldabra lily**. The two areas on Aldabra where the landscape is a little more gentle are along the fringes fertilized by sea-bird guano where gnarled **mapou trees** grow, and among the sand dunes in the south.

▼ *Below: Old graves of turtle-hunters and Chinese sea cucumber gatherers on Aldabra.*

Fauna

Birds, of course, are born to fly. The few flightless species around the world tend to be household names, with the solitaire of Rodrigues and the dodo of Mauritius perhaps the best known of them all. In the Indian Ocean, however, all are dead and gone, except for Aldabra's **white-throated rail**, the little olive green and rather tame bird that pecks about the bush. Rare, though rather unspectacular to look at, the rail is joined by the unique **Aldabra drongo**, with its forked tail, and the skulking **Aldabra warbler**.

In addition there are thousands of other **terns**, **tropicbirds** and **boobies** rising from the mangroves. The boobies are known as *fou* (daft) in Kreol, possibly because they are easily frightened into disgorging their catch by bullying **frigate birds** who breed in tens of thousands on Aldabra. **Flamingos** can be seen, as well as the striking **Aldabra sacred ibis**, while the **Aldabra souimanga sunbirds** are far more colourful than their granitic island cousins. The **Aldabra fruit bat**, with its distinctive white face, cruises in the evening among the trees.

▲ *Above: Boobies and frigate birds uniquely co-nest in the mangrove forests fringing Aldabra lagoon.*

THE ALDABRA GOATS

Among the incredible and unusual wildlife on Aldabra, the last thing you would expect to find is a plain old goat. The Aldabra goats are a throwback (so old salts say) to the days when the British navy would drop off a couple of the hardy animals, and perhaps plant a few coconut trees on remote islands so that shipwreck victims had some hope of survival when they drifted onto the inevitable desert island.

Possibly the strangest of all creatures on this living museum is the large **robber** or **coconut crab**. This reddish-pink, sometimes green monster, a land-breathing crab which can grow up to 60cm (2ft) long, likes to hide away under rocks and scuttle up coconut trees at night to rip open green nuts with its huge pincers.

The Aldabra Group

Cosmoledo atoll, Astove and Assomption Island are part of the Aldabra group. **Cosmoledo** is a 19km (12-mile) atoll broken up into 12 islands, whose reefs are littered with wrecks. Sailing close to the ring of islands can be hazardous as its landfalls (with names such as Wizard, Mosquito and Pagoda) are widely separated but linked by silent deadly reef. The harvesting of turtle, guano and green snail (mother-of-pearl) denuded Cosmoledo of much of its flora and fauna, although the atoll is still very attractive. A million pairs of sooty terns among other birds are the only inhabitants of Cosmoledo.

Dinosaurs

Although they can swim quite well, it is unlikely that the Aldabran tortoise came to the atoll from the Galapagos, halfway around the world and the only other natural habitat of giant tortoises. On land, they can manage 30m (100ft) an hour, but this unstressed attitude pays off, as they can also go for weeks without food, and have been reported to live for 150 years. The tortoise goes back to dinosaur days, a species even older than the Nile crocodiles that used to terrify early Seychellois settlers.

Astove is a ring atoll with only one break into its beach-lined lagoon. Centuries ago a group of slaves lived here in freedom for 40 years after their ship was wrecked on the atoll's reef. Today's few inhabitants eke out a living exporting reed brooms to Mahé.

Assomption, to the west of Cosmoledo and 27km (17 miles) south of Aldabra, is the staging post for Aldabra, with a newly constructed airstrip, and accommodation available. Once another great source of guano, these days its sand is highly valued by the construction industry on the Inner Islands.

FARQUHAR GROUP

Farquhar can occasionally be lashed with terrible cyclones that sneak across the Indian Ocean from the northwest during the months of January and February. Winds of up to 120 knots ('just beginning to turn me on' as Seychelles yachtsman Brownie will tell you at Victoria's Yacht Club) howl across the two largest islands and their great circlet of reef, whipping the palms and cutting a swathe of destruction like a scythe across the islands. Underwater the terrible convulsions of the ocean heave and crash the corals as if in an avalanche. No wonder that Farquhar (discovered

CORAL ATOLLS

One of Charles Darwin's aims during his circumnavigation on the *Beagle* was to determine the formation of coral atolls. His view (which is still widely recognized) is that atolls are the final stage of a continuing upgrowth of coral around a sinking volcanic island. Coral is also always growing outwards from the centre of an atoll, favouring the ocean-facing side where plankton is richer than in the water of the lagoon.

◀ *Opposite: Aldabra's mid-lagoon mushroom-shaped coral formations attract the attention of a snorkeller.*
▼ *Below: A yacht delivers visitors to remote Assomption Island.*

FRIGATE BIRDS

- Known as the pirates of the air, they live by harrying other sea birds and forcing them to disgorge or drop their fish.
- There are five species in the world, two of which have important colonies on Aldabra atoll.
- They are jet black, angular, almost stylized birds, with long wings and a distinctive forked tail.
- The male frigate bird has a red patch under its chin which it will inflate to impress its mate.

▼ *Below: Noddy ponders his nest for the night.*

in 1504 by João de Nova, the Portuguese navigator) and its neighbour Providence have the deadliest shipwreck record in Seychelles, some 12 in all. In the 20th century alone, Providence has been responsible for the loss of the *Jorgen Bank*, the *Endeavour*, *SS Syria* and at least one schooner, the *Maggie Low*.

However, make it past the treacherous reefs and strong currents of the narrow pass into the Farquhar lagoon, and it is one of the safest and loveliest anchorages in the islands. Farquhar is lush with palms and casuarinas growing down to white beaches. There is a settlement there, a phone, a seldom used airstrip, and a simple island house which can be rented to visitors through the IDC. The islands are 710km (440 miles) from Mahé.

The group takes its name from Sir Robert Farquhar, a governor of Mauritius, and in fact these islands were only transferred from Mauritius to Seychelles in 1921. Only Providence and Farquhar are inhabited.

Best Times to Visit

The granitic islands in particular have heavy rains in December and January. The coral islands receive less rain but it can be erratic with sudden, heavy showers any time of the year. It is less humid on the coral islands and there's usually a sea breeze. Bird-watching is best from April to October, fishing from October to April, and diving from March to May and September to November. Farquhar can suffer cyclones.

Getting There

Aircraft or helicopter transfers to and from the islands tend to be organized by the resorts, including the private islands of Alphonse, Anonyme, Bird, Cousin, Desroches, Frégate, Félicité, North, Denis Island and Ste Anne's.
Amirantes: There are 10 islands in the group. Flights to Desroches, or 24 hours by yacht. Contact the following yacht charter companies: Blue Safari, e-mail: bluesafari@seychelles.sc Elegant Yachting, e-mail: elegant@email.sc Island Charters, e-mail: info@islandcharters.sc Seafever Charters, e-mail: info@seafevercharter.sc Cruising the Amirantes by yacht is magnificent. Astove, Bijoutier, Coétivy, Cosmoledo, Farquhar, Platte and Poivre are managed by the Islands Development Co. (IDC). Incoming boats must apply for permission to visit: Port and Marine Services Division, e-mail: marineservices@

seychellesports.sc Due to the sensitive prawn industry there is no access to Coétivy.
Aldabra: *Indian Ocean Explorer* (info@ioexpl.com) can be chartered from November to April. There is an airstrip on Assomption. Seychelles Islands Foundation, sif@seychelles.net

Getting Around

The normal means of transport is to **walk**. Longer trips to the far side of the larger islands would normally be done by small boats with an outboard engine.

Where to Stay

Lodges or resorts are often the only accommodation on a particular island; generally they are small, luxurious, and exclusive.
Alphonse Island Lodge (Coralline), tel: 248 322682, e-mail: alphonse@seychelles.sc 30 thatched A-frames in Amirantes.
Bird Island Lodge (Coralline), tel: 248 323322, e-mail: reservations@birdislandseychelles.com website: www.birdislandseychelles.com 24 chalets.
Desroches Island Resort (Coralline), tel: 248 229003, e-mail: reservations@desroches-island.com website: www.naiaderesorts.com Superb diving.
Frégate Island Private (Granitic), tel: 248 670100, e-mail: info@fregate.com website: www.fregate.com 16 rooms, seven beaches. Luxury living for the bird and beetle boffins.
North Island (Granitic), tel: 248 293100, e-mail:

info@north-island.com website: www.north-island.com Villas, spa and connoisseur's cellar.
Denis Private Island (Coralline), tel: 248 288963, e-mail: info@denisisland.com website: www.denisisland.com 25 luxury villas, elegant lodge, lush forest, azure seas. Rates include drinks.
Hilton Silhouette Labriz Island, tel: 248 293949, e-mail: reservations@labriz-seychelles.com website: www.universalresorts.com Champagne welcome.

Where to Eat

All those islands with lodges have excellent kitchens. Other than boutiques in these lodges, there are no shops.

Activities and Excursions

Day trips by helicopter or boat, and occasionally by aircraft, are possible to some of the islands. Fishing, sailing, diving, snorkelling and nature walks are usually offered at all the islands with lodges.

Useful Contacts

Indian Ocean Explorer Cruises, tel: 248 225844, e-mail: info@ioexpl.com
Islands Development Co. (IDC), tel: 248 224640, e-mail: idc@seychelles.sc
Seychelles Islands Foundation, tel: 248 321735, e-mail: sif@seychelles.net
Nature Protection Trust, tel: 248 323711, e-mail: npts@seychelles.net

Travel Tips

Tourist Information
Seychelles maintains Tourist Offices in the following countries around the world, among others:
France (Paris), tel: 33 1 4453 9320, e-mail: info@tourismeseychelles.com
Germany (Frankfurt), tel: 49 69 2972 0789, e-mail: info@seychelles-service-center.de
Italy (Rome), tel: 39 0 6509 0135, e-mail: info@seychelles-stb.it
South Africa (Cape Town), tel: 27 21 551 5855, e-mail: seychelles@stoza.com
Spain (Madrid), tel: 39 41 702 0804, e-mail: info@turismoseychelles.com
UAE (Dubai), tel: 971 4286 5586, e-mail: seychelles@stome.ae
In Seychelles:
Tourist Information Office, Independence House, near Twa Zwazo roundabout, tel: 248 610800.

Air Seychelles
Air Seychelles has sales offices or GSA's in:
France (Paris), tel: 33 1 4289 8683;
Germany (Munich), tel: 49 89 5525 3338;
India, tel: 91 11 2335 0295, e-mail: kg@tracrep.com

Italy (Rome), tel: 00 39 06 509 8413;
UK (Crawley), tel: 44 1293 596 656/5;
South Africa (Johannesburg), tel: 27 11 781 2111;
South Korea, tel: 82 2 6399 6927, e-mail: consul@seychellestour.co.kr
Qatar (Doha), tel: 974 441 1414;
and in 37 other countries.

Entry Requirements
A valid passport is required but Seychelles does not require visitors to obtain visas. You will need a return ticket and a hotel booking. You will be given a numbered entry card stub which you must quote at your hotel and return to Immigration at the end of your visit.

Health Requirements
Nil. Seychelles is free of common tropical diseases, such as malaria, typhoid, cholera, bilharzia and yellow fever.

Customs
There is a duty-free allowance of 400 cigarettes and 4 litres of spirits or wine. Spearguns, firearms, agricultural products, animals and drugs (other than personal medicinal) are not allowed.

Travel to Seychelles
Mahé is the only port of entry. Air Seychelles flies from London, Paris, Rome, Johannesburg, Mauritius and Singapore. All yachts must contact the Harbour Master, e-mail: hm@seychelles.sc US military drones operate from Seychelles.

Travel in Seychelles
Car hire is best. The **bus** service is good but seldom extends beyond 19:00 on Mahé and 17:30 on Praslin. **Taxis** are plentiful but quite expensive. There are only three traffic lights in Seychelles (one at Praslin airport) and seriously hairy drop-offs on all mountain and rural roads on Mahé. **Bicycles** can be hired particularly on Praslin and La Digue. Air Seychelles has regular inter-island **flights** as does Helicopter Seychelles. Cat Cocos **catamaran** (150-seater) operates to Praslin and Mason's Travel catamaran to La Digue.

Clothes: What to Pack
Bring your swimming costume, a broad-brimmed hat, umbrella, sun barrier, dark glasses, binoculars, 2-pin adaptor and snorkelling gear.

Long trousers could be needed for the evening.

Money Matters

There is no longer exchange control in Seychelles. The Seychelles **Rupee** (around SCR12 to US$1, SCR18 to £1, SCR15 to €1) was floated on the open market in 2010 and the rupee is used everywhere. The Seychelles Rupee, which is divided into 100 cents, comes in denominations of SCR500, SCR100, SCR50, SCR25 and SCR10. There are **banks** with ATMs on Mahé, Praslin and La Digue; they are open from 08:30–14:00 and on Saturdays 09:00–11:00. Airport banks are open for some flights only. The black market used to thrive under strict foreign exchange controls but now is a thing of the past.

Tipping. Restaurants and hotel bills usually include a VAT charge, but a tip for good service is always appreciated.

Accommodation

Seychelles has a number of **large hotels**, usually on the best beaches on Mahé and Praslin, which are ideal if you are on a package holiday. There are smaller, more exclusive, hotels on Mahé, Praslin and La Digue. There are also a large number of 'Affordable Seychelles' **smaller hotels**, **guesthouses** and **self-catering** establishments which are the best way to pick up the flavour of the islands. Many book into these for three nights and then look around. There are luxury

'one-island-one-resort' **lodges** on the granitic Anonyme, Cousine, Frégate, Félicité, North, Silhouette and Praslin's Round Island but the best are such outer coral islands as Bird, Denis and Desroches. The government initially set a limit of 5000 hotel beds in Seychelles, a number which has been considerably exceeded. Prices range from US$130 (B&B for two persons) to US$4000 per night. Truly. There are **no camping facilities** anywhere on the islands and if you're on a budget, stick to the smaller or self-catering establishments and travel by bus. Essential to book your first hotel before you arrive (you will be asked at Immigration). The Central Reservations Office for visitors from Europe is in Paris, tel: 33 1 4021 2412, e-mail: contact@seychelles-resa.com website: www.seychelles-resa.com Nearly all hotels and guesthouses serve excellent meals, and there is a wide selection of **restaurants** mainly concentrating on Kreol and French cuisine. Seafood dishes predominate. Count on US$40 per person. Cheapest takeaway is about US$4.

Trading Hours

Shops and businesses are closed on Saturday afternoons and Sundays, although some rural shops open at odd hours over the weekend and late in the evenings. Normal business hours are 09:00 to 16:00 with a one-hour break, 12:00 to 13:00, when some will shut.

GOOD READING

Accouche, Samuel: *Once Upon a Time, a Soungoula*. (1976) Folk Tales.
Amin, Mohammed et al: *Aldabra*. (1995) Superb coffee-table book.
Bradley, John: *A History* (1940) 2 volumes. Everything about old Seychelles.
British Navy: *South Indian Ocean Pilot*. (1971) Essential for yachties.
Brown, James: *Adrift*. (1981) True story novel.
Bulpin, TV: *Islands in a Forgotten Sea*. (1969) Travel.
Burridge, Glynn: *Voices: Seychelles short stories*. (2000)
Grimshaw, Brendon: *A Grain of Sand*. (1996) A Robinson Crusoe life.
McAteer, William: *History of Seychelles*. (2002) 2 volumes.
North, Marianne: *A Vision of Eden*. (1993) Victorian botanist and artist.
Skerrett, Adrian and Judith: *Beautiful Plants of Seychelles*. (1991) Also bird books.
Tingay, Paul: *Night of the Rukh*. (1975) Adventure novel.
Travis, William: *Beyond the Reefs*. (1959) True diving adventures.
Veevers-Carter, Wendy: *Island Home*. (1970) A family alone on Rémire.

Measurements

Seychelles uses the metric system throughout.

Communications

Cable and Wireless have provided Seychelles with a superb **telephone**, **fax** and **e-mail** system, albeit the telephone directory is not fully comprehensive. There are payphones everywhere (usually using cards which can be purchased at Cable and Wireless, post offices, and other general outlets). GSM has a **mobile network** plus roaming. Mobile starter packs are available from C & W and Airtel (airport, tel: 600600). Paradise FM supplies the latest pop music while SBC broadcasts **TV and radio** in Kreol, English and French. The Nation is the official daily, and the independent Regar comes out on Fridays. Seychelles stamps are colourful and often treasured by collectors. There is a philatelic bureau at the main post office near the clock tower in Victoria. The international code for phoning Seychelles is 248.

Operator, tel: 100; **International Operator**, tel: 151; **Directory Enquiries**, tel: 181; **Emergencies**, tel: 999.

Time Difference
Seychelles time is GMT + 4.

Electricity
240 AC; 3-pin (square) plugs.

Medical Services
There is an excellent **hospital** at Mount Fleuri, near the Botanical Gardens, with X-ray, pathology, and all facilities, tel: 388000. Private **dental services** are also available, tel: 224852 or 224354. There are **small hospitals or clinics** at many of the little villages on Mahé, Praslin and La Digue.

Private medical doctors include: Dr KS Chetty, tel: 321911 and Dr H Jivan, tel: 324008.

Pharmacies:
Foch Heng, tel: 322751 (after-hours tel: 241233); Behram's, tel: 225559; George Lilams, tel: 322336. The hospital dispensary opens Monday–Friday from 08:00 to 16:00, and Saturdays from 08:00 to 12:30

Optometrists, tel: 321993 or 321177.

Emergencies
Ambulance, Police, Fire, tel: 999; Hospital, Mount Fleuri, Mahé, tel: 388000.

Gay Travellers
There are no gay clubs in Seychelles, but the Seychellois choose not to betray any homophobia.

Health Hazards
Sandflies are a real problem on some beaches, especially on those with seaweed lying heavy on them. They are minute and itch like crazy. **Do not** underestimate them. Use a preventative cream or lotion such as Bushman Ultra (80% Deet). **Slippery surfaces** – marble, granite, even manmade wooden decks in hotels can be deadly after rain. Seychelles has no malaria but does have **dengue**. Air conditioning can lead to colds as you acclimatize. Fans are best for mosquitoes. **Sunburn** can ruin your first few days, so be careful. **Coral scratches** should be treated immediately as they quickly become infected. Wear trainers when walking on exposed reef or in seaweedy or grey sand water, but also watch where you walk. **Sea urchins spines** should be removed if they come out easily, but left if they don't. As with **jellyfish stings** and **stonefish poisoning**, immerse the area in the hottest water you can stand. This will help deactivate the toxin, and then seek medical advice. Under no circumstances pick up

	CONVERSION CHART	
From	**To**	**Multiply By**
Millimetres	Inches	0.0394
Metres	Yards	1.0936
Metres	Feet	3.281
Kilometres	Miles	0.6214
Square kilometres	Square miles	0.386
Hectares	Acres	2.471
Litres	Pints	1.760
Kilograms	Pounds	2.205
Tonnes	Tons	0.984
To convert Celsius to Fahrenheit: x 9 ÷ 5 + 32		

large and 100% deadly **cone shells**. The ugly **stonefish** that lurks in sand underwater is highly poisonous but rarely encountered. **Centipedes** and **scorpions** are very rare. **AIDS**, as everywhere else in the world, is also found in Seychelles.

Security

Violent crime is rare. Seychelles is a fairly wealthy country. Bag-snatching is almost unheard of. Petty theft occurs on some beaches, now patrolled by police. Lock your car. Many hotels have safes. Resorts on some islands deliberately have no keys to indicate security. Central Police Station, Victoria, tel: 288000.

Women Travallers

Avoid obvious risks like walking about alone at night or swimming at a deserted beach. Bus travel is perfectly safe. Topless is fine on the beach.

Smoking

Only where there is no roof above and no walls around you. Or underwater.

Language

Kreol, a language mainly derived from French (but written phonetically and therefore difficult to decipher at first from its French origins), is the main language. But English and French are also official languages. Italian and German are understood by many tour operators and

hoteliers. With visitors from the Middle East, South Africa, and Russia, it is hardly surprising that Arabic, Afrikaans, Malayalam, even Slovenian are increasingly heard in Seychelles.

Sports

The following are all available in Seychelles:
Golf. Reef Golf Club Hotel, tel: 376251, or Lémuria, Praslin (18-hole, championship) tel: 281281.
Tennis and Squash. Many of the hotels have courts. Try Plantation Club, Le Méridien Barbarons; also National Sports Council Courts in Mont Fleuri.
Windsurfing. Try Beau Vallon Bay, Mahé Beach Hotel, and Côte d'Or, Praslin.
Riding (on the beach and water only). Le Méridien Barbarons, tel: 673000; also on La Digue.
Sailing. The Yacht Club in Victoria welcomes temporary members, tel: 322362. Enquire there or at the neighbouring Marine Charter for details on chartering boats, tel: 322126.
Diving (and learning to dive). Underwater Centre, Coral Strand Hotel, tel: 621000. As well as this centre, there are many others.
Deep-sea fishing. Marine Charter, tel: 322126.
Waterskiing. Various hotels offer waterskiing, as do operators at Beau Vallon Bay and elsewhere.
Surfing. Sometimes the surfing is good at Grand'Anse in

Mahé. Not many boards are available in Seychelles.
Paragliding. At Beau Vallon Bay. Beach operators.
Walking. There are a number of marked trails on Mahé and from the Coco de Mer Hotel on Praslin and on La Digue. Leaflets and guides are available.

Nightlife

Katiolo's (south of the airport) is the favourite nightclub, Deepam's Victoria the only cinema, and there are several casinos. Large hotels have dinner dances at weekends, usually with Kreol dancing floor shows.

Websites

Tourism:
www.seychelles.travel and
www.masonstravel.com
Hotel Listings:
www.the-seychelles.com

PUBLIC HOLIDAYS

New Year
1 and 2 January
Good Friday
Easter Sunday
Labour Day 1 May
Liberation Day 5 June
National Reconciliation Day 18 June
Independence Day 29 June
**Assumption Day
(La Digue Festival)**
15 August
All Saints Day 1 November
Feast of the Immaculate Conception 8 December
Christmas Day 25 December

INDEX